LIFE IN RHYTHM

Life in Rhythm

Become Your Best Without Burning Out

Terry Williams

Published by Game Changer Publishing

Paperback ISBN: 979-8-90158-100-1

Hardcover ISBN: 979-8-90158-064-6

Digital ISBN: 979-8-90158-065-3

www.GameChangerPublishing.com

To Ashley

Thank you for being my person. You believe in me more than even I believe in me, and while you appreciate, support, and empower all that I am, you also encourage me to continue leveling up. Because of you, I am forever in pursuit, growing into my best self. I am in awe of you, and being your husband is my life's greatest gift.

To Terry III, Trenton, and Rhys

Being your dad is a priceless blessing. While I aspire to live a life that teaches you great things, I must say… ironically, the greatest things I've ever learned are things I've gleaned from you. Legacy is funny like that. Life talks back to us. As I marvel at all you're becoming, it enhances my journey in becoming. My heart swells with gratitude at every thought of you. I am immeasurably proud of you and your biggest fan always.

ADVANCE PRAISE

"My NFL career wouldn't have lasted 7 years without connecting with Terry Williams to train during the 2017 off-season. My 2016 rookie year with the Philadelphia Eagles was so bad, I genuinely didn't know if I'd be playing much longer. I believe it's no coincidence that the very next season after training with Terry, not only did I get baptized the night before a game, but I was also on the first Super Bowl-winning team in Eagles franchise history. That season changed my life in the best way, and it wasn't possible without Terry. I give that brief flashback to say this book is what Terry naturally embodies. It's what he taught me long before any of the words were written on paper. The path in these pages shares a gritty and challenging truth that sustains us through life's inevitable wins and losses. This book is for the men and women who understand that success doesn't happen by accident. It's for those who know that real purpose is a lifelong journey of new discoveries that can't simply be found in money or countless career accolades. It's for those who can accept that real growth happens at a marathon pace and are willing to run in rhythm."

— Marcus Johnson, Super Bowl Champion

THANK YOU FOR BUYING LIFE IN RHYTHM!

In appreciation, I have a gift for you.
Scan the QR code to access a free video masterclass, applying every concept taught in the book:

LIFE IN RHYTHM

BECOME YOUR BEST
WITHOUT BURNING OUT

TERRY WILLIAMS

FOREWORD

Terry Williams doesn't just coach performance; he guides people into who they are truly called to be. This book isn't another quick fix or passing self-help trend. It's a genuine invitation to live with clarity and purpose. It poses the deeper questions: *How are you living? How do you show up? Who are you becoming right now?*

With more than a decade of experience as both a certified strength coach and neuroscience coach, Terry has a rare ability to weave together physical health, mindset, and identity. He has spent years helping others cultivate not just strength, but a richer understanding of themselves. His approach, anchored in grace, grit, gratitude, and growth, reminds us that transformation requires time, honesty, and compassion.

One of the signature frameworks in this book is Terry's ENVIVO model: Endeavor, Neutral Mindset, Values, Interests, Vision, and Outcomes. It's more than theory; it's a practical tool for alignment.

Through it, he equips readers to live with intention and make choices rooted in vision rather than pressure.

I've witnessed Terry embody every principle in these pages. He has walked alongside professional athletes and everyday individuals alike, always with patience, wisdom, and care. He doesn't push growth; he cultivates it.

On a personal note, Terry is one of my best friends and was a groomsman in my wedding. His speech on my big night reminded everyone of the power of legacy, love, and living with purpose. That moment captured his essence: a man who speaks truth with love and practices it daily.

Professionally, I've seen his impact firsthand. At our NBA National Strength Coaches Association event in Chicago, he led our group of coaches through a core values exercise that dove far deeper than the surface. He didn't simply facilitate a conversation; he created space for a level of vulnerability and connection our coaches had never encountered before.

This book carries the same spirit. It is thoughtful, practical, and deeply inspiring. If you're ready to move forward, not by doing more, but by becoming more, these words will meet you where you are and help you step into greater clarity and peace.

Terry, I'm proud of you. You've poured wisdom, truth, and care into these pages, and I know they will impact lives in transformative ways.

– *Willie Cruz*
Director of Athletic Performance, Houston Rockets
2025 NBA Strength Coach of the Year

CONTENTS

INTRODUCTION

Have you ever had a day when you woke up, and everything just seemed right in the world? Where your mood aligned with your to-do list, productivity came easy, and you even had a little time for self-care and leisure when the work was done?

Prominent voices in the world of sports psychology would call this "flow state," an effortless rhythm that drives one toward ultimate success. It comes with calm confidence, a mindset rooted in perfect peace, an immunity to the pressures of the moment, and the ability to deliver results flawlessly, often with swagger, too.

These seemingly perfect days are rare jewels, but they don't have to be. Our lived experience is, to some degree, influenced by our daily choices. Finding a flow state is easier when we seek purpose and choose growth. By dialing in core elements like our nonnegotiable values, a clear vision for the future, and an understanding of what endeavors we are willing to devote our life's work to, we can extend grace to ourselves and others, show up with grit, lead with gratitude, and lean into growth.

Finding this rhythm can be hard when we're unaware of our life's natural cadence. In this book, I'll walk with you in figuring this out. To be clear, these pages are designed to impart wisdom and make room for independent thought. It's not a rigid rulebook, nor is it rife with one-size-fits-all maxims.

I've won big, failed catastrophically, and made myself a home in the messy middle, understanding now that wins and losses are both temporary. You may come to feel freedom in understanding the same.

I don't claim to be a guru, an expert, or a know-it-all. I am simply a person who leads from a position of learning, generously sharing my takeaways along the way, hoping you can hear a bit of your story in mine and that it better informs your process as you write a new and wonderful story. Everybody deserves to live a life worth telling a story about, and it's my honor to chart a bold course with you toward that end.

Rhythm is what drives music forward, yet it is also what it always returns to. Ironic, isn't it? Purpose is a rhythm. One who leads a family feels compelled by their love for those they share a home with to leave that home daily and do good work in the world. Then, as the workday draws to a close, that same sense of purpose drives them back home to give sweet snuggles to the humans (and/or fur babies) they've spent the day laboring to provide for. They may not love every element of their work, but life would feel as if it's missing a beat had they not undertaken a path to purpose in providership.

In the same way, growth is a rhythm. It's a delicate dance between the person we are and who we dream of becoming. If purpose is the foundation, growth lays the bricks. Understanding both allows us to build a better house to live in.

One area where I had to learn a healthier rhythm to achieve optimal results is in my running. As a long-time coach, I've worked with athletes in many fast-twitch sports, serving as a conditioning coach to NFL, UFC, and NBA athletes. Endurance sports were never in my wheelhouse professionally, though they were of interest to me personally. In my HYROX training, I've learned to become a skilled distance runner, as it plays a huge part in race preparation and performance.

I remember talking with friends at the gym about how I was fighting to increase my running pace. I'd tell them how hard I'd worked on speed training, but that it seemed not to be yielding any improvement. Sensing my frustration and offering help, one client challenged me politely: "You know, the world's fastest runners spend a lot of time running slowly."

Lightbulb moment!

I checked my ego as a coach and went to see someone else. It was time to *be coached*. This humility healed me. My running coach doesn't care that I've founded gyms and led fitness communities. To him, I was a student of the egoless pursuit of running, and frankly, one who needed *a lot* of help.

In total confirmation of what I'd heard that had led me to him, he told me that running slowly gets you faster, while running fast gets you injured. He proposed I adopt an 80/20 rhythm: 80 percent of my weekly mileage would now be in "zone two." This is the pace where my heart rate is low enough, and my running speed is slow enough, that I can hold a conversation or sing a song. I could still hit the track for speed days and mix it up with some fun interval runs, of course, but never to the tune of more than 20 percent of my miles.

This coach further explained that by slowing down, I was building a stronger aerobic base. My body was becoming more efficient at processing oxygen, buffering off lactic acid, and ultimately, forging itself into a stronger biological machine. Like the laborious task of building and installing pistons for the engine of a car, future speed is being supported long before a gas pedal is pressed.

Amazingly, it worked. Imagine that!

I spend more time running slowly on my daily training runs and now have a wider base built to support higher peak performance. Every race lately has been a new personal record. Every year, I age backwards, running further and faster, because I've embraced a more sustainable rhythm. When I obsessed over speed, I killed any chance of gaining speed. When I honored my body, submitted to leadership, and adopted a new approach, the thing I was seeking found me.

In the pages ahead, I'll be your coach. Not an arrogant voice of correction, but a kind guide offering connection. I'll welcome you in as a student and get you up to speed quickly. Together, we'll explore a more sustainable and fulfilling life, lived at the pace of peace. We'll talk about rigor, rest, and the rhythm between them.

Nothing in this book is heady or heavy. With intention, it's designed to flow like a candid conversation, presenting stories, questions, and actionable insights. I recommend not reading more than one chapter daily, allowing space to pause, reflect, and embody these learnings. It's time to learn how to go further, faster. Let's trade your reckless striving for restful striding. Welcome to Life in Rhythm.

PART ONE
SEEKING PURPOSE

Of all the existential questions a human can ask, one seems the basis for all others: "What's my purpose?" It makes sense that we would carry this curiosity, as purpose is tied to identity. If we have an understanding of our life's big assignment, we are confident in all of life's little decisions.

Said another way, if we know more clearly who we are here to be, we have a playbook that guides us on what we are here to do. Where we live, whom we choose to pursue relationships with, the types of education and career paths we build for ourselves, and even simple things like where we spend our time and what hobbies we pursue can be shaped by an understanding of our life's impact on the world.

Understanding your purpose is like holding sand in your hand. Surely, you can get a grasp of it, but holding it is never passive. You watch what's in your hand curiously, as it's alive yet inanimate, moving, sifting, and slipping through your fingers without your effort or permission. You can be sure in one moment that you've got a secure grip on it, and then feel challenged beyond your capacity when the winds of change blow and you notice some of this understanding leaving you instantly, in ways you can't just pick up again.

There are times, too, when it rains at the beach. That is to say, everything you hold gets drenched and soggy. You may not enjoy the process of enduring the storm, yet oddly, you come to appreciate it later because you find that your sand has caked into something more solid, less fickle, and easier to hold.

For the person pursuing purpose, certainty is a myth, and adversity brings clarity. Hold yourself as lightly as you hold this shifting sand. Let it change shapes a million times, never doubting its presence because you feel it, see it, and hold it, even as it doesn't always play nice.

In the chapters ahead, we'll explore purpose through a framework I've developed, called the ENVIVO method. This term finds its roots in Latin, meaning "in the living" or "in the body." In modern Spanish, it refers to live action in film or stage productions.

Put simply, this method doesn't focus on what you *theoretically* or *metaphorically* believe to be your purpose, but rather what you are actively embodying in a moment. It reflects what you are truly living out right now and what a camera would capture if it objectively observed your daily activities.

The letters in ENVIVO each represent a tenet of the purpose formula, making it easy to hold as a reminder. Revisit this simple expression any time the wind blows, and you need to check in with the sand you hold. The pieces of this process are:

Endeavor: Doing a hard thing, honoring the art of delayed gratification.

Neutral mindset: Not falling to the negative, nor being naively positive. Choosing action in adversity.

Values: Creating a list of the things you wouldn't trade for material wealth. These things *are* your wealth.

Interests: Simply stating what you'll spend your time doing.

Vision: Forming a clear understanding of your imagined future.

Outcomes: Understanding your desired impact and releasing attachment to control.

After gaining clarity in these areas, you'll have a framework for intentionally adopting a new viewpoint, with room for questions without threatening your sense of self. In this freedom, you'll form a healthy outlook on what it means to be you, and from there, we'll dive into how you grow this newly understood you.

Enjoy the journey.

CHAPTER 1
ENDEAVOR

You need a hobby that kicks you in the teeth.

Time and time again, I find this principle to be true in my life and profoundly impactful as I lean into it. We unlock good things by repeatedly honoring hard things.

Our idea of purpose comes from both nature and nurture. That is to say, we are first introduced to a worldview by our parents, peers, or people of influence. We are told a story about what makes a life purposeful, and as our own lives present tests, we find that we either choose to accept or challenge these theories as we press in to conquer what is set before us.

Forming an idea of purpose rooted in a story you write for yourself is a powerful experience, unlocking new levels of meaning and bringing a true sense of fulfillment. As wild as the idea sounds, you don't have to be shocked by the inconvenience of a bad break to grow in grit, forge resilience, or find purpose. You can select for yourself a hard thing to do on a regular basis, which grows your purpose muscle, rep over rep. This adds new levels to your understanding of your own strengths, enabling you to respond more effectively when a difficult time arises in your life.

Acclaimed author and podcaster Jefferson Bethke calls this phenomenon an "unrelenting endeavor," noting that what makes this type of practice special is that it forces you into a space of honoring delayed gratification.

In an unrelenting endeavor, you find yourself showing up time and time again, putting in an amount of labor that is invasive to your comfort and schedule, to meet yourself more deeply. You can do it correctly every day and still not see quick results. The moment you get it wrong, you experience instant consequences.

It feels unfair to endure the grueling process, yet you find yourself feeling oddly optimistic about the outcome. While you can't ensure your success, you see it as a possibility worth fighting for. You find yourself researching routines and asking questions of every expert you have access to. You learn that ChatGPT cannot solve this puzzle for you. You'd give anything to get 1 percent better at this thing. You've fallen in love with this craft and now treat it like a marriage. Though it can be frustrating at times, you stand firm in your professed commitment to it, prioritize it, and work to become your best self in support of your relationship with it. This is something someone could coach you in, but no one can do it for you.

An unrelenting endeavor can be something common like gardening. Others see you tending to your garden and only notice the fruits, though you grapple with the roots. Your rosebush is fragrant, sprawling, and teeming with vibrant color, bringing a simple and refreshing joy to your home's curb appeal.

To make this possible, you've had to toil in the soil. You waited through cold winters before making it to every easy spring. You reconciled sky-high water bills, researched every fertilizer known to man, and learned about new types of predatory pests you never knew you'd lose sleep over. To produce a pretty thing, you've been digging in a dirty thing. Some roses have died, while others have bloomed, and you're still honing the art of discovery on your way to mastery.

Perhaps in your life, it's the pursuit of fitness. The workouts are painful, but you resolve to push through. No single session, by itself, leads to six-pack abs, but you see the value in suffering well. You find yourself living into the long process that, over time, introduces you to your more fit self. This, in turn, welcomes you to deeper levels within the practice: eating cleaner, sleeping more, investing in worthwhile supplements, and even dedicating entire training sessions to stretching or mobility work to prevent injury and support your grind.

What does the unrelenting endeavor look like for you?

The best example I've ever seen of this is the life and work of my good friend Matt Schnell. Matt is a professional mixed martial arts athlete, well known for his success in the UFC. I was introduced to him by another athlete I worked with in my strength and conditioning days, and I felt humbled and honored to become a small part of something big: supporting his fight camps as he went on a tear, holding a top-ten spot in the flyweight rankings for years.

A menacing and perpetual threat to the crown, Matt's mindset was absolutely dialed. He was the rare type who savors every rep mindfully. He didn't just do the work he was asked to. He asked questions about the type of work we'd do and shared his own ideas about how we might optimize the workflow (even when it meant the sessions would be significantly longer and harder).

At the end of our all-out suffer-fests, he'd thank me for the work. He would pause, look me in the eye, shake my hand as if he genuinely appreciated the investment, and, with fervor and humility, express that he'd enjoyed the push. He felt sincere gratitude for the brutal work being doled out in a warehouse without air conditioning on Southeast Texas summer afternoons, with cruel temperatures soaring well above 100 degrees. There would often be pain, and there would occasionally be puke, but the man never missed a session.

Matt hails from Louisiana, which consistently ranks at or near the bottom in economic stability, measured by GDP, among all U.S. states. It also ranks between 47th and 49th among the 50 states in education, according to the United States Census Bureau.

Though I was born and raised in Houston, I'm a product of my Louisiana Creole lineage. After learning the rich history of my grandparents and hearing the against-all-odds stories from aunts and uncles at family cookouts, I'm very familiar with the storyline of coming from the bottom, finding a lane of endeavor in under-resourced circumstances, and making a living out of it that affords one's kids a better life than they've had themselves. I knew all too well that legacy moments were born in deficits.

Though this was a coach-client relationship on paper, this was a brotherhood in practice. I could understand his story and chosen path at a level that seared a deep respect into my mind. I found myself diving deep into an endeavor of my own in support of his. I'd not only coach drills but also join in. My body, though ten years older than his, worked hard to hold pace in a worthy manner.

I'd then step into a weekly rhythm of Brazilian jiu-jitsu and kickboxing, spending my "off days" experiencing firsthand the sport-specific demands Matt would face. I didn't just want to be his guy in the gym but also his dog in the trenches. Occasionally, I'd be spotted by coaches in fight training spaces where I intended to just attend a class, and I'd be asked if I minded going a few rounds with one of the local pros preparing for a fight. In a game of honor, you always accept the opportunity. You show up to the endeavor, and the endeavor finds you. The work doesn't ask permission; it just shows up with the expectation of your readiness to dance.

Matt would say the darndest things in media interviews. He'd also say similar things mid-workout. Simple truths that felt like they came from the book of Proverbs would effortlessly pour from his mind into the room he was in, bringing light into the space and shaking awake the dreamer in every person under the sound of his voice. Gems of insight came to the surface with ease.

He never once guaranteed a victory. He always showed humility. He'd comment on "the little lies" we learn to believe that influence our self-discipline. He spoke very candidly about his fears and how, when he was most confident, he'd get caught slipping, but when he could properly harness a healthy sense of danger awareness, he could "hand out a scared ass-whooping."

My all-time favorite Schnell quote came just before his best fight to date, when he said, "I didn't have great prospects. I was never the star student. Everything I have I've built with my own hands." He followed this with "Fifteen focused minutes. Anyone in the world."

Shortly after these words were spoken, he was caught in the deep end of a one-sided fight. He'd lost the first round badly. He was taking serious damage in the second round as well. Surviving multiple shots that dazed and froze him, Schnell trucked on. Announcers marveled at the fact that he was still conscious, and one nearly stammered words that would suggest the fight was over. Thankfully, he course-corrected mid-sentence, because what he almost said would've implicated him in a lack of journalistic integrity. It ain't over till it's over.

In stunning fashion, Matt "Danger" Schnell caught his foe slipping, seized a split-second opening, and landed a dramatic comeback that instantly earned the respect of the all-time greats in his game. He emphatically climbed out from under his opponent's limp body on the canvas and made the "money rub" hand gesture. Smile. Swagger. Sweet success. This would be his second consecutive time earning the coveted "Fight of the Night" bonus. ESPN went on to call this showdown "the greatest comeback win in UFC history."

Think about that… An unrelenting endeavor puts you in a position to dare to lose, to humbly and honorably pursue a thing even to your own detriment, and to give your life to something in pursuit of fifteen minutes. In those fifteen minutes, you can be put to shame famously on national television, with every beer-bellied blogger in America relishing in your defeat, or you can become legendary. It takes the rigor and the risk to know the reward.

Remember, your endeavor doesn't have to be this epic. Plant the garden. Take up singing lessons. Learn to cook. Begin the work you said you'd do toward that real estate license, or just find a hobby that reminds you that it's okay to be bad at something for a while. Sit with struggle and come back for more.

Accept that the "J curve" is a real thing. Neuroscientists note that when we pursue something new and hard, we can expect our formation journey to take the shape of the letter "J," initially dipping down woefully and producing things like doubt, debt, and defeat before eventually rising wonderfully to produce things like grit, gratitude, and growth.

Our first pillar of purpose is endeavor. It's about finding a craft and taking a chance. It takes embracing the discomfort, releasing attachment to achievement, and finding joy in the journey. I'd rather be in the waters knee-deep, away from the safe shore and wading in losses, occasionally being knocked off my feet by waves of utter failure, as I continue walking toward the deep unknown, than be limited to the predictable experience of those relaxing on the beach.

PAUSE AND PROCESS: Take a moment to journal what landed for you here.

What ***endeavor*** will you take on, and what do you hope to learn from it?

CHAPTER 2
NEUTRAL MINDSET

Own your losses; seize your wins.

At the age of eighteen, Mary Earline Jubert arrived on the campus of Lamar University as an unsung hero in the civil rights movement. Born to a struggling African-American family in the segregated South, she'd always wanted more for herself than what the world offered her. She noticed there was a ceiling on her prospects that others weren't trapped under, and she would see to it that boundaries were pushed, limits questioned, and dreams explored. A charismatic challenger of norms, she wasn't driven by rage or indignation but rather an insatiable zeal for life and achievement that couldn't be arrested by the laws of social order.

Nobody would talk her out of pursuing her dream of becoming an educator, and to make that dream a reality, she needed... well, an education. Throughout her childhood, schools had been divided by race, and she had been marginalized. She couldn't accept this as a foreshadowing of her future and wouldn't stand for any reduction in her options for pursuing a degree.

Brown v. Board of Education, the Supreme Court case that declared segregation unconstitutional, was decided in 1956. This was serendipitous timing, she thought, as she reached college the following semester.

However, these were also dangerous times to go dabbling in disruption. Despite this ruling existing in principle, it did not have popular consensus nor widespread acceptance from the institutions it implicated. There were still eight more daunting years until the eventual passing of the Civil Rights Act of 1964, and anyone who dared to challenge the status quo would surely be subjected to unspeakable horrors.

Even her own family advised her not to go to college, partly because it was the customary and sensible norm in that day for Black children to stay near home and help the family, and partly because, as much as they loved her and wanted to see her fly, they legitimately feared for her life.

Mary did what makes her who she is. All advisement be damned, she went for it. She became a member of the second-ever integrated class on a university campus in the state of Texas. Many historians studying the Civil Rights Era believe that, had brave souls not acted during the loophole period, we would never have seen the requisite pressure applied to the system, paving the way for the eventual Civil Rights Act and the subsequent journey toward a more expansive equality. She would encounter vitriol and endure violence daily. Picket lines outside of her classes would feature signs saying things like *"race mixing is communism"* and issuing epithets, death threats, and other verbal morbidities.

Mary Earline would go on to live her dream as an educator, serving for thirty-one years in a district where minorities comprised the majority, climbing the ladder from teacher to principal, and also supporting mental health and social safety outcomes as a counselor during her tenure.

The thick skin and resilient heart she formed in her old college days paid off, as she would later encounter treacherous battles in her adult life, too: the loss of a son, far too young; the loss of a breast to cancer; the loss of autoimmune health to vitiligo, a condition ironically manifesting itself in the discoloring of skin pigmentation, clinically believed to be linked to chronic stress. She owned her losses, and she fought to claim her wins, nonetheless.

I didn't have to rummage through the annals of biographical history to source her story. I was blessed to receive it in the same way I received her famously top-secret gumbo recipe: around a table, over a hot meal, in person. Mary Earline is my paternal grandmother. This sweet soul is my hero. Her presence as a revered matriarch in our family feels larger than life.

I may be the only person carrying forward her recipes, but I am far from the only one carrying forward a legacy of learning and leadership. Among her grandchildren, all have bachelor's degrees, one holds a master's degree, and another a Ph.D. Her courage to enter a war zone has elevated her lineage through pervasive intergenerational impact. She smiles in adoration, humbly appreciating and openly honoring the people now walking out what she once was told couldn't be done. Her ripple effect has destroyed forces that were systematically built to limit human potential.

A conversation with Mary Earline is one hell of a ride. She maintains, "Every day is a good day," but she doesn't see the world through rose-colored glasses or paint a positive picture of everything. In fact, she can explain in vivid detail some of the most humiliating and horrific happenings, yet she still holds room for hope. She also knows that hope is not a strategy. She speaks to an action-oriented approach that doesn't brush anything under the rug, and yet she unshakably believes in doing what's best. It's like hope is the gasoline, courage is the steering wheel, and ***action*** is the engine.

She is convinced that God is good when life is bad, that she holds the autonomy to change what she refuses to accept, and that tomorrow can be joyous even as yesterday was not. Her laugh is contagious, her smile is angelic, and her exuberant emphasis in storytelling is marvelous. She is a bundle of vibrant, enthusiastic glee. I don't think it is possible to share a table with her without being convinced that you are capable of changing the world.

Her mindset has taught me this: when you're willing to work toward a solution, you always have one within reach.

The late mindset coach and bestselling author Trevor Moawad devoted his life to understanding mental frameworks like this and termed the phenomenon "neutral thinking." It's themed by a radical ownership of what has not worked out in the past, coupled with an undaunted belief in the possibility of a favorable future, ultimately connected to a call to do something proactive *today*.

As we journey in seeking purpose, imagine what this kind of unalterable mindset can unlock in your life. Purpose unbroken: the ability to absorb any loss and continue fearlessly forward to claim your greater win.

Trevor's research happened before his eyes in real time. He served as a brain trainer for elite athletes and coaches, most notably working with Russell Wilson during his Super Bowl championship run and with Nick Saban during his historic tenure as the greatest college football coach of all time.

Trevor had to watch through nail-biting moments as his clients faced seemingly insurmountable odds in tight scenarios: razor-thin margins for error, the clock ticking toward a dooming zero, managing complicated emotions. He had the unenviable job of holding to the belief that his principles would manifest, channeled through imperfect humans, to produce history-making outcomes.

He was right.

In most cases, he found that people who could make peace with the past were able to forgive themselves for the mistakes that led to the dire situation and let go of animosity toward teammates, referees, or unexpected circumstances that hindered performance. A person who knows they can win will even free their mind of malice toward those rooting for them to lose. These elite performers could also hold space for the belief that they always had one more move and that, if properly stewarded, they could excel.

A clear mind is a superpower. A rolling boil brings too much heat, disorienting steam, and an unsteady surface that erases any hope of clarity, but in the still waters of a calm mind, you can see your own reflection. The best in the world can do this. Impervious to pressure, they can kill the boil, remember who they are, and take charge of the most unsettling situations.

Let's break down this neutral approach in simple terms.

- Own the past: It happened. It was bad. I can't undo this, and I choose to accept it.
- Lean into the future: I believe the future can yield a positive outcome.
- Act in the present: I have the gift of opportunity right now. With the right execution, I can win.

Third-party research from the National Institutes of Health corroborates these claims, suggesting that mindset reframes are no fluke. The NIH found that teams with a neutral mindset tend to demonstrate higher winning percentages than those with default negative or positive mindsets. They can focus on facts rather than feelings (logic over bias), leading to improved decision-making and ultimately increasing performance and the likelihood of winning.

Imagine what might've happened if Mary Earline had allowed herself to stew in a default negative mindset. Nobody could have blamed her. It was wise to avoid fighting for a total overhaul of the system, and her family earnestly believed she should do so. But it would've led to a searing loss. In her old age, she'd regret not earning the degree she wanted, and perhaps my generation would have lacked inspiration from being raised in the lineage of a trailblazer, preventing us from chasing dreams and becoming achievers.

Now imagine the opposite. Sadly, if she'd had a passively positive mindset, assuming things would "just happen to work out," she would've stepped into a hell on earth with no game plan and been quickly overcome by the powers that be. Perhaps in that scenario, I would've never had a shot at coming to be, nor would the pages you are reading now.

The truth is, while positivity is important, it cannot be achieved through wishful thinking. You mustn't only believe that positivity is possible but also that your will to act is the womb from which it is born. You have to produce it.

Now let's zoom in. What does a neutral mindset look like for *you*? It can feel inspiring to read about its outcomes for others, but it is no easy feat to carry against your own odds. The tool of reframing mindset is one you'll need to keep with you, using it as often as necessary to stay on track toward your goals. Letting this tool go unused and become dull over time would mean that you slowly shift into powerlessness and accept mediocrity as your lot in life.

Maybe you've found yourself stuck financially. Maybe it's a complicated work environment that torments your days or a rocky familial relationship that keeps you up at night. Whatever pushes you to the brink of your sanity, be it the desire to escape a bad situation or the dream of entering a beautiful one, know that the pain you carry is valid. You are worthy of wrestling with this and are likely handling it much better than you think you are.

The human mind is fickle behind closed doors. Even the person who publicly presents as supremely confident, when doing the brave work of being alone with the feral self, is prone to experience those *Am I enough?* questions from time to time. It's human nature. The brain does this by design with the kind intention of protecting us.

The amygdala, a gland located near the brain's center and just above your ears, is triggered by emotion. It will quickly send you into a state of alarm when it senses a situational threat, driving your nervous system into what we call the sympathetic state, also known as "fight or flight." This can freeze you in negative thought patterns and stifle your ability to take meaningful action.

But get this: the amygdala doesn't know the difference between you being triggered by an offensive, politically charged Facebook rant and you being at risk of getting hit by a bus. It requires you to choose quickly between rioting and retreating when it detects a threat at *any* level.

This information system was vital when humans knew simpler times. Imagine being a caveman and hearing rustling in the bushes. Your brain's job was to instantly put you on high alert for the potential of a saber-toothed tiger so you could quickly feel the fear and follow it with a rapid response. Whether you liked it or not, if you wanted to live, it was instantly time to hunt or hide.

The prefrontal cortex, by contrast, is driven by logic. Located near the front of the brain behind your forehead, this is your brain's CEO. It's the seat of sound reasoning, decision-making, and executive function. When it's activated, it can send your nervous system into the parasympathetic state, also known as "rest and digest." The challenge is that in high-stress situations, it can quickly be driven offline. When the fire alarm sounds off in your head, your brain would rather call 911 than call the boss to have a meeting about it. This makes perfect sense.

When faced with a challenge that feels overwhelming, it's as if the brain experiences flooded pathways between the amygdala and the prefrontal cortex. There is no way for our car of reasoning to commute from emotion to logic. So, we must "pause and process." We've got to first recognize and accept the feeling, without judgment, and nurture it patiently. Then, as the proverbial storm ends and floodwaters subside, we can slowly and safely make the drive to decision-making from a more regulated space.

Now let's dive even deeper. There's a fundamental difference between the brain and the mind, says Dr. Daniel Amen, a renowned psychiatrist and trusted voice in neuroscience. He explains that, while the brain is a physical organ built for processing information and steering bodily functions, the mind is your driver for the abstract elements of your thinking and feeling self, guiding processes like willpower, memory, consciousness, and belief. It stands to reason, then, that nothing is broken in us when we feel stuck in our situation. Our brains *should* protect us.

The power of a neutral mindset is that after we first process a thought, we can choose a belief. You can empower your mind to talk back to your brain. What wonderful news! With enough awareness, you can thank your brain for sending safety signals, acknowledge your nervous system for the bodily sensations of tension and jitters, and inform these systems that, while you appreciate their support, you recognize that this threat is not fatal, and you choose to believe a different narrative. You can give the fight-or-flight response permission to relax so you can rest and digest. Your regulated self is then not chained to what hasn't worked in the past or what appears doomed in the future. You become fully present.

If you spend too long ruminating on the past, you'll be met by sensations like shame, regret, or depression.

If you spend too long ruminating on the future, you'll be met by sensations like worry, fear, and anxiety.

If you can process a thought and choose a belief, you'll enter the present accompanied by the sensation of peace.

Let's make this practical. Here's a three-step process:

1. **Process the thought:** Hold a funeral for your feelings. Pause and welcome the pain. Don't judge it; allow it. This isn't weakness; it's a natural human experience.
2. **Choose a belief:** Declare what you believe to be possible as a winning outcome and own it. Genuinely accept this imagined outcome as fact. Take time to feel gratitude for it, as if it were already here.
3. **Notice the rifts:** Allow your mind to second-guess your belief a thousand times. Don't fight, deny, or judge this act of nature. Simply notice the rift and kindly invite your mind back to belief. Send as many invitations as you need until you notice a subtle, gradual shift toward a steady stance in your spirit.

Mary Earline on campus. Saban on the sideline. You in the rut life has handed you.

Accept that even if the past was trash, the future can be treasure, and there is something you can do about it… right now. When you are willing to work toward a solution, you always have one within reach.

PAUSE AND PROCESS: What challenge feels big for you in life? How will you reframe your mindset to neutral? What would become possible for you if you didn't sell out to the negative or the passive positive, instead taking action from a space of poise and peace?

CHAPTER 3
VALUES

"Say yes to things eternal."

These are borrowed words from my wife, Ashley. She has a delightful radiance about her and a charming way of capturing big ideas in a few small words, helping me sort the mess in my mind and find peace in a values-based rhythm.

I still remember the first time I heard her mutter the expression. It immediately resonated in my soul. I could feel its meaning and couldn't unsee the beauty in it. In this context, "eternal" could be taken to mean ideals we can pass down for generations, always seeing them compound and grow in the good they produce. Things eternal are things you don't just believe with your mind, but you carry in your spirit, too. These are the priceless things you just know in your bones you're supposed to be about and proudly represent in the world.

I sometimes find Ashley saying she needs to sidestep a professional obligation to honor a personal conviction. Ironically, many times, the thing she thought she'd have to fumble ends up working itself out anyway, showing up in perfect timing.

Things eternal are core values, and core values are a compass. The values you hold to be eternally true will point you in the direction of your best self and have a way of giving you an answer before you've even been presented with the question.

For Ashley, I've seen this show up in some pretty inspiring ways. She would say of herself that she's a "recovering workaholic," which makes sense as she's a former Wall Street investment banker, founder or COO of multiple businesses, and married to me (I'm a real piece of work). Yet I've seen her, in a moment of professional urgency, drop everything at a moment's notice to be with a grieving friend. I've seen her rearrange days riddled with deadlines and disasters to chaperone our kids' field trips. I've seen her exemplify what it means to "know your no," regardless of consequence, to make room for the bigger "yes."

Like Ashley, we can all benefit from gaining a clear understanding of our core values. This brings our lives into a confident cadence, never letting us drift too far from our truest selves. In the pages ahead, you'll notice that we're about to take a workshop approach to mining for values. This isn't the kind of thing you can carry textbook knowledge of, and far too many of us carry the simple "faith, family, fitness, and fun" model, regurgitating platitudes rather than sitting in stillness and studying what's truly "eternal" for you.

Find a silent space, quiet your mind, and let's explore. It's time to learn how to determine what deserves your "yes."

VALUES PRACTICE #1: LAND YOUR LIST

We're getting into a contemplative process here, so get comfortable and set your space for a distraction-free time of welcoming wonder. Maybe you remove your shoes or explore this over a hot cup of coffee. Feel free to occasionally close your eyes and visualize, soften your gaze as you reflect on these ideas, or pause from the book to make space to process and think through this piece. Whatever you do, don't allow that glowing rectangle that lives in your pocket to be present while you walk through this exercise.

All cozied up? Cool. Let's do it.

Take a moment to imagine that sitting on a table in a peaceful, uncluttered space are four fragile glass spheres. Paper-thin and delicate, these clear balls are sure to shatter if dropped. Zero chance they'd bounce, settle, and remain intact. They are sized so that you can only hold three in one hand at one time, and when you do, managing the load feels risky. Visualize yourself holding these three glass balls in one hand, with no allowance for using your other hand.

These three balls represent a short list of your core values.

The fourth ball, left unclaimed on the table, represents $10 million. Cash. Tax-free. Ready to hit your account ***today*** if you can pick it up.

Visualize yourself struggling to find a way to secure the fourth ball in the same hand without dropping a single ball you already hold. Notice how it would feel to risk shattering (irreparably destroying or forever losing) any of these items you ascribe worth to.

Think about three things that are so precious to you right now that the additional dream of financial wealth suddenly seems worthless by comparison.

Question: What do you see yourself holding that you refuse to lose, driving you to reject the moneyball and take joy in all that remains in hand?

These three things are what you wouldn't sell your soul for. This is your truest form of wealth. These are your values.

VALUES PRACTICE #2: APPLY YOUR ANSWERS

Let's take a trip and bring these values with us, shall we?

I love hiking. It's always hard, yet it's always incredible. This paradox finds its moorings in the truth that we spend our time in work and life seeking to "get away," yet have the propensity to feel a bit anxious when we've gotten far enough off the grid that we lose cell service and a trail route appears unclear. We sought adventure, but we forgot how thin the air is at elevation and how our quadriceps burn when climbing. But on a mountaintop, the stunning view is worth the hard-earned miles we logged on the ascent. Nothing is proven worthy until it's seen a valley and a victory.

Reflect on a mountaintop moment. We're talking highlight-reel material for your life. On a mountaintop, the clouds are your carpet. You're standing in sunshine even if there's a storm. You can't see the strife below because the only things at eye level here, above the clouds, are other majestic peaks.

What's the tallest peak you've stood on? Perhaps it was a time of academic or career achievement, a moment of bliss in a relationship, a family win, or long-awaited good news you received unexpectedly that changed your life. Looking back on this moment, what values do you recognize as being present in you as you welcomed the unbridled joy?

Sit with this for a while.

Next, reflect on the opposite: a valley moment. Now we're talking hardship. Sometimes you're not on a mountaintop, and in fact, you have a mountain in your way. On the rugged earth here below, you're under the dark shadow of surrounding peaks even on a sunny day. And should a storm roll through, you're a sitting duck, subject to the elements. You've got more than wet socks to worry about if things pick up, because there's no shelter in the wilderness.

What's the deepest valley you've found yourself in? Revisit the pain and don't fight it. Simply be with it. When have you felt alone, lost, and defenseless? When did it appear that losing was your lot in life and winning was not within reach? Looking back on this moment, what values do you notice were present? What characteristics or ideals did you find yourself leaning into during this hard time in hopes of turning it around and making it to higher ground?

Take a moment to sit with this.

Is there a relationship between the values you landed in practice one and practice two? There's no right answer. You may have had your list widened, or you may have noticed the second practice reaffirming your notes from the first. Either way, select exactly three values from the above practices. We'll challenge them in this final step to mine for total clarity.

VALUES PRACTICE #3: CHALLENGE THESE TRUTHS

For each of your three remaining values, simply ask, "Why?" five times. This process, originally developed by Japanese inventor and industrialist Sakichi Toyoda, establishes a simple system for identifying root causes. Drilling down on the "why" brings more meaning to the "what."

Note your values, then play a game with them, allowing each "why" to drop a level deeper, adopting a conversational tone, and responding to your previous answer. For example, if I say I hold a value of "family," my five whys practice may look something like this…

Name a value: Family

- *Why family?* Because I love my wife and kids. And my parents, too. I love to see them as grandparents.
- *Why do they mean so much to you?* The idea that I fell in love with someone and we co-created people we love is amazing. And we, the products of our parents, now *are* parents… so mind-blowing to me.
- *Why does the concept of parenting stand out to you?* I'm grateful to my parents. I now understand them better as an adult. I hope I can be as good as they were and that my kids can understand my deep care for them.
- *Why does your impact as a parent mean so much to you?* Because I want my family to grow better with each new generation. I want my kids to be better parents than me, too, producing even better grandkids I get to someday meet.

- *Why does it matter how your grandchildren turn out?*
  Because legacy matters to me deeply.

See what happened there? The five whys took me from cliché to crystal clear.

In this example, love of family is rooted in the idea of legacy. I dream of being an incredible father, someone who raises kids who are empowered by my parenting and become incredible parents themselves, producing compounding levels of good humans produced in my family line.

This value points to gratitude for a past generation, hope for a future generation, and an understood urgency for purpose-driven action in my current generation. The idea of legacy, then, is a clarifying guide, pointing me to my best self.

If I encounter a fork-in-the-road moment of indecision, I can ask my core values to answer for me. Do I take this job or that one? Perhaps one better positions me for time with my kids. Should I take the day off from training? Well, I guess I could, but it's clearly the better legacy move to be the healthiest version of myself for my family. Whichever direction I ultimately go, legacy is kept in mind.

What does this practice look like for you?

In the same way that my wife says, "Say yes to things eternal," I often find myself saying, "Life talks back to you." Interestingly, these two statements go hand in hand, revealing a deeply compelling truth. When we learn to say yes to our values and what we find to matter endlessly, we find confirmation along our path in the everyday, ordinary moments. In the same way that some things are triggers, reminding us of our past trauma and threatening to drive us into reacting as our lower selves, others show up as glimmers, reminding us of what we find to be beautiful and welcoming us to respond to life as our highest and best selves.

This happened to me once while I was lying on the table of a tattoo parlor. My right arm is coming together slowly and wonderfully as a mural sleeve that tells a story. Bit by bit, I'm having Gabriel Massey, a widely revered man of the craft, etch onto my arm some vivid images that represent stories of deep meaning, which I'm overjoyed to carry with me for life.

One day, as he was dialing up the gnarliest fern on my forearm, "G" glanced up over the top of his iconically retro black-framed glasses and asked with sincerity, "So, how's business?" We'd had many a chat about the gifts and the grief of small business ownership, so I knew I could be candid in my response. I didn't sugarcoat it. I told him of a big challenge our brand was facing at the time.

Suddenly, the buzz of the gun stopped. He paused the project long enough to school me with simplicity, saying, "You know, the older I get, the more I realize that I have no excuse to be miserable. It's all about ego death. Most things are not as dire as they seem in your head. They probably won't happen, and if they did? It wouldn't be the nightmare you've made it out to be in your worrying. Think about what you can move toward as you look for reasons to be happy. Gratitude. Service. Connection. If you look long enough for reasons to be happier, you *will* find them."

Mic drop.

And then he buzzed on, rattling away at a gorgeously detailed gradient in the fronds of this image he was blessing me with, which, ironically, represents the art of giving back to others while honoring one's own process of growth. The fern doesn't only draw sustenance from its soil as all plants do; it also deposits nutrients back into the soil across its life span and even in its dying, priming the grounds for more lush life.

Notice what happened here. G didn't sell out to pacifying comfort, nor did he downplay the hardship. He sat with me in the wreckage and shared practical wisdom. In doing so, he said words that reinforced for me exactly what my values are.

Gratitude. Service. Connection.

These words, as it so happens, are the ones I've carried as my three core values ever since this interaction.

Perhaps after completing the values practices and landing, applying, challenging, and reshaping your big three, you'll also observe life talking back to you. You may notice as you carry these values that suddenly you experience them being reinforced in passages of scripture, referenced in an overheard quote, or mentioned in a book, movie, or conversation. These are the guiding voices of truth, affirming you on your journey toward showing up at your best and brightest in this life.

On the other side of that coin, it's important that you also know that not every voice attributed with wisdom aligns with your values. For any chosen perspective, you can always find a talking head on TV or a guru on social media to push the point. Some are toxic and some trustworthy; our information conduits are a mixed bag of vice and virtue. If not rooted in your values, you'll accept any route that feels good and call it truth. Only after getting solid on who you are and what you wouldn't sell your soul for can you truly know what messaging echoes your values back to you, confirming that they're a safe source.

I was recently reading an incredible book written by a man who has achieved superhuman feats of endurance and grit. I marvel at his stories of mental toughness and unbreakable confidence in the tightest of situations. But among all that I can honestly say I admire in this figure, I also noted that he mentioned forgetting his wedding anniversary and foregoing family vacations.

In one story, he said he took his kids to a movie theater, set the little ones up with Icees and popcorn, then kissed them on the foreheads and said he was going for a quick five-mile run and would be back before the movie ended. This made my stomach drop. While I try my best not to judge others' behavior, I do notice when something I'm observing sets off an alarm in my spirit. This is life talking back to me, imploring me to choose a different path than what I'm seeing modeled. I can say objectively that such behavior doesn't align with "connection," one of my big three core values.

This person feels empowered by the thought of prioritizing training over all else, as it means he's singularly and supremely focused on his endeavor, and his spouse supports it. While he feels this teaches his children the value of toughness, I respectfully disagree. I don't say this to position my values as a rival to his, nor am I preaching my values as a model for you to follow. What I am saying, though, is that it's important to understand your values so well that you aren't easily influenced by all voices. You've got to spot the misalignments and edit the list of voices you welcome in to coach you on your journey.

If I know that I view the world through a different lens than someone else, I have two jobs here. I must not only hold gratitude for what I find right and true in what this person and I share but also note where my full agreement would compromise a value or cross a boundary.

In contrast, I once read a book by the late Dave Hollis entitled *Get Out of Your Own Way* that shook me to my core. At one point in his career, he was an executive vice president at Disney and a tour manager for Beyoncé, yet this husband and father of four maintained a personal policy of ending every workday at exactly 5:00 p.m. No matter what was at stake professionally, he held the line personally, remaining committed to spending time with his family daily.

Given the values I've shared, you can see how this narrative resonates more for me and why I've chosen to follow voices like his more closely. Tragically, Dave passed away at the young age of forty-seven, not long after releasing his life-changing literature. He couldn't have known at the time of taking his firm, values-based stance that the days he favored his family were indeed some of his final days. I'm sure his children are now deeply grateful that he chose them over the star-studded work he was pursuing. Our time is limited, so we may as well invest it in our values.

After establishing your values and scanning the world for messages that reinforce or rival them, it's important that you put them into action. It would be a travesty for them to become idle relics, collecting dust, as they're written on a sheet of paper, thumb-tacked to a wall. Values, like tattoos, should be carried with you for life. When you exercise them daily, challenge them regularly, and rely on them over the long haul, you begin to understand that life is about who you are becoming.

The most practical way to live your values is to connect them to habits.

Take a moment to consider three habits you'd like to eliminate. Don't even label them "bad"; just acknowledge that they don't serve you. Next, name three habits you'd like to add to your life. Don't label them "good," as we're not assigning morality to them. Own that you want these things added to your life. Now pair each of these habits with one of your values. Something magical happens when we do this. It loads the train, which will now carry you toward the person you dream of becoming. Talk about acting with purpose!

Habits are autonomic behavior patterns we get stuck in. Your brain decides what you'll do in response to a certain stimulus before you are even consciously aware. Much of this is based on what you've done before. However, according to brain science, neurons that fire together wire together. You can retrain your habits to take you in the direction of your values. Every rep you put in, pushing back against old patterns and putting in the work to build new ones, makes it increasingly likely that your future self will become adapted to automatically choose the things the current you dreams of picking up.

Your life is like a train, thundering so swiftly down its tracks that nobody is safe standing in front of it. This train is virtually unstoppable, either fast-tracking you straight to your destiny or driving you, quickly, further from your goals every minute.

As James Clear, author of *Atomic Habits*, puts it, "With healthy habits, time is your ally. With unhealthy habits, time is your enemy." The time will pass either way. You may as well be venturing in the direction of the life you seek. Value-aligned habit patterns are golden.

PAUSE AND PROCESS: What are your big three core values, and where will they steer your life?

CHAPTER 4
INTEREST

Garbage men have the best job on earth.

Truly, waste management professionals have a pretty sweet gig. Muse with me on this idea. They get in, get the job done, and get out… like ninjas. No customer is attempting to micromanage the manner in which they move the bins, load the truck, and navigate the neighborhood.

But you know who *does* notice their presence? Kids! The most joyful subset of the population is also the people group most prone to smile and wave at the teamsters. (This is what they call their units. That's dope, too.) These guys don't wear capes, but they do save the day. They make an average of 4.9 lbs. of waste per person in the U.S. disappear daily while we're away at work. Their routes are clear-cut, and they have a singular focus. They likely experience a lot of fulfillment from the fact that they are legitimately doing good for the community.

Pause and imagine for a moment what it would look like for your waste management solution to no longer be present. How would you feel suddenly needing to find a solution for where to send your putrid waste or how to transport it to its place of rest? How would trips to a landfill twice weekly impact your schedule? How many bags would pile up on the side of your house? Would you need a pickup truck to haul the refuse without sharing space with it in your vehicle?

Okay, so maybe we should reframe the opening sentence of this chapter. It may not be something we ourselves would consider to be the greatest gig if we had to take on the experience. Still true: Perhaps, we too, should begin smiling and waving at these guys. Their impact is huge!

While we're at it, let's look at happiness. Teamsters tend to report favorably high rates of workplace joy and life satisfaction. Unlike many people, statistics would indicate that these social servants actually *like* their line of labor. According to the United Nations Environmental Programme (UNEP), teamsters experience depression rates at about half the frequency and severity of the average American professional, and one senior-level teamster's salary is nearly 86 percent of the national median household income, meaning that if paired with a spouse's salary, a teamster is likely living an above-average lifestyle in terms of income. Not a terrible situation.

Now, let's unpack all this with perspective. Young aspiring professionals don't necessarily view the teamster role as a dream job. It's likely not on anyone's bucket list. Many in this line of work report that they were led to it by circumstance, as opportunity presented itself. That's fair, and it's awesome they've found a role by chance that can feed a family, reduce stress, and provide a communal, team-oriented atmosphere that fuels feelings of well-being.

Having an "interest" is broad like that. Your interest is the thing you intentionally pursue for an extended time horizon to give and receive value. It's not a hobby or a thing you dabble in to assess your willingness to commit; it's the thing you decide to go all in on as a means of bringing some form of good into the world. It's not the endeavor we spoke of in a prior chapter. It shows up as a job, such that what you pour your interest into can bring compound interest back to you in income and experience.

As we explore these pillars of purpose, consider what *interests* you. Don't limit yourself to what you dreamed of as a kid, what you think will give you the biggest paycheck, or what you feel makes you look impressive on your LinkedIn profile. Consider the good you can do in the world, attaching no judgment to the wild ideas that come up for you. Am I recommending that you pursue a career in waste management? No. Am I challenging you to think outside the box, in a lane other than your current role, and free from all preconceived notions? You bet.

One effective way to frame the idea of career interest with purpose in mind is to examine another "I" word: *ikigai.* This Japanese expression translates to "a reason for being." The ikigai framework has four purpose-aligned ingredients, helping you to mull over what completes your matrix, lights you up, and feels like a comprehensive path to fulfillment through the work you do.

Skill: What am I good at?

Passion: What do I enjoy doing?

Contribution: What good do I want to do in the world?

Income: How do I get paid to do it?

The idea is that with a strong enough understanding of what you like and are good at, and a heart to do it for the good of others, you can set yourself up nicely to gain reward. What you collect in a check is aligned with what you contribute to the world, and your conscience feels as good as your bank account.

Doing the work of landing your interest may seem like a waste of time if you're already deeply entrenched in a career path, but it can be refreshing to do this digging. You may discover that the role you presently have, and that you happened upon years ago, now makes all the sense in the world as it unearths a newfound understanding of why you chose it, why you were divinely connected with the people who took a chance in hiring you, and why it feels like a resounding confirmation of your reason for being.

Or perhaps you determine that your interest lies outside your current field, presenting an opportunity to pivot with purpose. Perhaps you find yourself between jobs, unsure of where or how to begin again. Nailing down a lane of interest means you now have an arrow directing your path, a guidepost for where to look next as you seek to build a new and enjoyable chapter.

If there is one thing I have a strong interest in being, it's being open. The one thing I do not want to be is rigid. Let's explore these themes for clarity.

Lao Tzu spoke with such reflective wisdom in studying the comparative character of rock and water. He notes in the *Tao Te Ching* that water is fluid, soft, and yielding, while rock is rigid. He's illustrating the point that what we see as firm, solid, and strong is brittle and therefore can break from, and become fragile when exposed to, consistent force over time.

Water, on the other hand, is formless. It can shapeshift to fit any container and even break said container when needed to remain in a state of flow. Every canyon is a literal monument to the tremendous power of water, which has fiercely carved its way through solid rock, forming an awe-inspiring geographical wonder in its wake.

Your chosen lane of interest works in a similar way. While copy-pasting your present-day role as an interest can answer the question and save you the work of introspection, it's rigid. A business closure, a surprise round of layoffs, or an opportunity elsewhere can shake your sense of security.

Similarly, answering quickly based on what you dreamed of being as a kid can be limiting. As you'll read in a later chapter, I have personally allowed my inner child to have a voice in informing my interests. This can be wonderful, but only within proper measure. While it can be inspiring and grounding, the goal is to ensure that it's not limiting. Allow the dreams of yesterday to help you see a clearer tomorrow, but don't cap the work at the age of that young dreamer, who would later learn and experience priceless things in continual becoming. Sit with it. Dare to be courageously curious. Become formless. Find the flow. Ask the bigger question... Maybe it's not about a specific profession, company, or industry. It might be about a chosen and heartfelt desire to release a particular kind of good into the world, which can then be reverse-engineered to identify fields that fit it.

Stay broad. It's absolutely fine to have a corporate job that doesn't sound "woo-woo" and "special" if it empowers you to be aligned with your best self and do your best in service to others. It's wonderful, also, to pursue the role that makes you happy without it being the thing that makes your parents proud or your peers impressed.

Doing this work may direct you with pinpoint accuracy to a clear and specific career path. Great! Now you know where to look, but not because you were rigid; more because your complex questions led you to a simple answer. Or you may find that, like one of the most affluent and connected people I know, your area of interest is broad and offers many options.

I know a person who is in sales. He's just flat-out good at it and has a big passion for conversational connection that generates leads from laughter. His genuine smile makes him a good fit for it. The stuff he sells totally elevates the operations of the businesses he serves. Because he's a game-changer for the folks he's called to serve, his job has become a game-changer for his family and lifestyle. He earns well because his interests are aligned.

He's not rigid in his role. He could lose this job, transition into a new industry, and sell a new thing. Remaining formless, he could easily apply his skill in a new setting. His values outside of work are hunting, cooking, and being a world-class dad. His job offers him the funding and freedom to spend plenty of time in the great outdoors, sourcing ingredients, and indoors with his sweet family, preparing incredible meals. Does his hunting game tempt him to start a career in hunting? Nah. Does his skill for cooking coax him to think about launching a restaurant? Nope. These things alone do not complete the puzzle of alignment for him. They're the sweet spoils of a career lived out from a clear understanding of his big interest.

Okay. Enough talk about that. This is a nuts-and-bolts chapter. Less reading, more reflection. Take ten minutes to sit in silent solitude, mindfully considering what lights you up.

What area of interest really inspires you, regardless of where this bold and sometimes scary question leads you? The answer will steer you in the direction of your purpose.

PAUSE AND PROCESS: What is your big, broad interest? What sorts of career paths might enable you to use this gift to do good?

CHAPTER 5
VISION

Remembering the future brings joy in the now.

It was an absolutely perfect afternoon in Vancouver, British Columbia. I'd just finished speaking at the annual fiscal-year kickoff meeting in Lululemon Athletica's global headquarters. I found myself seated next to their president and several members of their senior leadership team. I glanced down at my feet, not in an attempt at mindfulness or present moment awareness, but to admire my sweet kicks once again. They'd gifted me their first-ever men's shoe before its release date. I couldn't believe it.

I then glanced out of a window, marveling at the immaculate view. From the eleventh floor of this contemporary office space turned production site, I had an unobstructed view of the North Shore mountains and the pristine waters of the Burrard Inlet. My coffee, which had been too hot to enjoy before speaking, had now cooled to the perfect temperature. As I sipped it, I savored it. I was in no hurry to be anywhere but here, and I noticed every flavor note instead of mindlessly sucking it down on the wish that today's caffeine would magically hit me harder. This slow rhythm felt a lot like heaven.

There were no looming meetings, and there was no urgency to check my email. I did notice one text come through from a friend who'd just seen my piece on a live stream, but I received the notification as a cue to tuck my phone away and enjoy the magnificent moment. I resolved to go with "do not disturb" and catch up on all communications later.

I began to see even the unseen clearly. I thought back on every moment in my relationship with the people behind this brand that had led to this mountaintop moment. I thought about the many events they empowered in our gyms back home in Texas. I could see the moment they popped up at our run club ten years prior and asked me to become an ambassador. I revisited the moments when they showed up as allies in socially divisive times, empowering my voice to speak on behalf of marginalized people and to raise awareness for causes connected to love.

Then I arrived at the image that would forever live rent-free in my head: I reflected on the photograph that had been featured on the screens just minutes before as an illustration while I spoke. In this photograph, a four-year-old Terry, or "TJ," as my family called me in my infancy, stood before a Christmas tree, decked out in a sweet '80s powder-blue Houston Oilers replica uniform with red-and-white accents. TJ was flashing the cheekiest, squintiest, most fervent full-body smile through the wide face mask of a helmet far too large for even the biggest-headed boy.

Every time I see this photo, whether literally or in my mind, I feel that same sense of unbridled joy again. I feel my inner child rejoice when I'm reminded of a time when my life was simple. I'd asked for a specific thing on a wish list and then received it as a gift.

Oh, to bring that simple satisfaction into adulthood, right? We hustle. We feel pressure to produce. We live to work, with the dream of reaching a status, someday, where we can simply work to live. We've forgotten about the longings we carried as children and never pause to think about whether what we're currently pursuing would bring that child a full-body smile.

The image was a visual aid for the people I presented to that day, but I have no doubt it spoke to me more than anyone else. I thought about how, when I was four, I didn't know the first thing about football. I didn't understand the rules of the game, nor was I the kind of kid who craved contact and intensity. But I loved the vibe. I loved to visit the Astrodome with my parents. The fries were salty. The aura (and mustache) of star quarterback Warren Moon was inspiring. The energy of thousands of people converging to represent the city and root for the team was intoxicating.

I'd be willing to bet that when you were four, you didn't know how to spell the word "limitations," nor did you understand what it meant to be "realistic." What did you want to be before bills were a thing? Before title and position mattered? Before you were told to "grow up"? What would you have said you wanted to be when you grew up? Let your mind play in this space.

In a moment far from home, I reflected on that Oilers jersey and how it had shown up in my life's path over the years. By this time, the Oilers had two offshoots: the Tennessee Titans, formed when the team relocated to Nashville in '97, and the Houston Texans, who brought rebirth to Bayou City ball in 2002. I smiled at the irony as I thought about the fact that I was serving as an off-season conditioning coach to a player for the Titans and how I'd made several appearances for the Texans for opportunities like speaking at Rookie Day, Homecoming Weekend, and my all-time favorite, Father's Day, and occasionally training a few of the guys.

It's unreal how our early dreams show up in unlikely ways later. We feel like it's a coincidence, or just the way the ball bounces, but I believe it's bigger than that. When we set a vision clearly, everything in our subconscious begins looking for confirmation, and everything from our hobbies and interests to our selection of friend groups to our eventual landing spot is influenced by this. This marks a direct path between our early dreaming and our eventual doing.

There's a principle in neuroscience that's most simply explained by the phrase "You spot it, you got it." Think of a person who deeply inspires you. What human, dead or alive, would you go to dinner with if you got just that one evening together? One rule: this person must be older than you if they are still living. This is an individual who has seen a lot of life and poured it out for others in a special way. This could be anyone from a world leader to a celebrity to a family member who is no longer with us. No limits. One meal, one person, anyone you'd like.

Pause and bring that person's face clearly to mind. You got it? Great. Now consider this... Forget about their name, career, and status. When it comes to Superman, the cape is cool and all, but *flight* is the superpower. As renowned MIT lecturer Peter Senge says, "It's not what the vision is. It's what the vision does." What character attribute does this person carry, or what value do they reflect that inspires you? Bring this, too, clearly to your mind.

Now, here's where it gets good. According to what social scientists currently understand about the workings of the human mind, inspiration appears to reflect possession. This means that what you are drawn to is a reminder of what's already in you. It's almost as if what you are reaching for, you are unconsciously carrying in seed form. You were moved by this person's impact because God wove into your purposeful design the ability to sow something similar into the world. This person isn't just your hero; they're your divinely appointed reminder of what you're called to be. Studying their life and being stirred emotionally by all you discover literally wakes up potential in you, as if their life bears a blueprint for yours. To be clear, you must live your own story. But in the pursuit of that, having a model to follow is a powerful tool.

How much more would you stay on track toward living your purpose if you carried with you two important figures: your younger self and your elder hero? The current rendition of you would find moments of crystal clarity and total presence, at peace with the moment, finding beauty in it, and marveling at sweet reminders from a younger and an elder guide that confirm you're on the right path. There is immense power in vision.

Let's take this one step further. It's time, right now, to develop a whole new vision for your life, with the current moment being a launchpad. Your childlike wonder today brings you that cheeky smile of fulfillment tomorrow.

To envision, you must first have "in vision." Doing the work of introspection is key, and this framework has some striking unlocks. Before we continue, prepare your space, making it uncluttered and unbothered, free of digital distractions. Complete this exercise when you have the time to get quiet, empowering you to live loud.

Hold space for a moment of disconnection from all stressors and heavy thoughts. If it serves you well, you may even consider putting this book down and setting aside a separate moment to continue, perhaps after a good run or in the early or late hours of the day when you have the luxury of solitude. You'll want a clear mind, a calm heart, a regulated nervous system, and the ability to dream without "limits," "maturity," or being "realistic." Bring the best you to this moment.

In this practice, you will look back from a future date to today, honoring the past you've built and celebrating the wins you're grateful for along the way. This paints a clear picture of what you'd like to do, have, and be as you lean toward the noted future date. The result is a clear vision map.

When you're ready to begin, set a timer for four minutes or play one low-stimulation song without lyrics. Spending more time invites a loss of focus or a spiral into overthinking. In the space provided here or on a separate notepad, answer the questions in this exercise. Don't second-guess your thoughts and feelings; just let them flow.

Remembering the future.

Today's date is ________________ (note the date exactly twenty years from today).

Where am I today? Who am I with?

____

____

____

What's on my agenda today that will sharpen my mind, body, or spirit?

Over the past twenty years, what personal accomplishment am I most proud of?

What looks different in the world due to my contributions?

Whose life have I changed, and how?

Over the last twenty years, what's the biggest problem I have solved?

____

____

____

Of the many things that are true and present in my life today, what brings me the deepest joy?

____

____

____

Knowing the answers to these questions frames a path to purpose for you.

Now let's do the hard work of bottom-lining it. No room for wordy explanations. You get just two words to encapsulate the wonder of what you've envisioned for your future so that you can easily draw it down as a mantra to guide your life decisions today. One adjective followed by one verb or noun. That's it.

Don't put any pressure on yourself to fully capture every answer. Simply grab two words that are sufficient to remind you of the wonder you dream of, so they can ally with you in moving you toward your destiny.

Here are some examples to help you get your juices flowing:

- **Adjective-noun coupling:** Unbridled fun. Resilient

community. Unshakable confidence. Perfect peace. Hard-earned clarity. Empowering generosity.

- **Adjective-verb coupling:** Restful residing. Carefree giving. Bountiful receiving. Ceaseless laughing. Communally thriving.

Now it's your turn.

My two-word vision statement:

____

____

Excellent. You now have words that frame the work, a manner of carrying and communicating what you thought you were reaching for but, in fact, already hold. It's now easier to sow the seed to serve the eventual harvest. Life will bring you sunshine and rain. Both help this seedling break through the soil. Live your vision, pursue your purpose, and trust the process.

One helpful hack is to keep these words where you can see them. Remember, "You spot it, you got it." If you keep the vision in front of your eyes, you plant the vision in your mind, which then tattoos it on your heart.

I love how one passage from Habakkuk 2:2–3 makes it simple. One translation (MSG) reads, *"And then God answered: Write this. Write what you see. Write it in big block letters so that it can be seen on the run. This vision-message is a witness, pointing to what's coming. It aches for the coming. I can hardly wait! And it doesn't lie. If it seems slow in coming, wait. It's on its way. It will come right on time."*

My goodness. Vision has never felt clearer. Write these words plainly and boldly and keep them in sight. Lean into them as a coming truth. You might sticky note them to the left or right of the mouse pad in your MacBook, print them out and tape them to your bathroom mirror, jot a note to fold into your wallet, create a fun background image on your iPhone, or even make a printable sticker to affix to your steering wheel. Hold these words. View them daily.

There are endless ways to reinforce holding to a vision and making it plain. If you're a visual person, there's always the classic vision board. Extra points if you make it a vision party and do it with friends. Maybe you also carry an image of your chosen dinner party hero or a photo of your younger self as a reminder.

Lastly, maybe there's a physical item that speaks these words to you clearly. I've kept a small ceramic sculpture of a longhorn skull, painted with beautiful designs, which was on the nightstand in the hotel room Ashley and I stayed in on our wedding night. This item is more precious to me than any luxury good you could offer and is something I'll still have in my possession on my dying day. It makes my vision clear. It represents every commitment I made that day and what I strive to live by every day. It reminds me of the immense fulfillment that comes with long-term commitment, through highs and lows and all the ordinary in between.

However you decide to note your vision, I hope you'll continue to behold it as you put in the reps to become it. I also sincerely hope that one day you will come to know a tranquil and unforgettable moment, looking back on the now, enamored by an incredible view, and absolutely shaken by the way you are living what you once envisioned.

PAUSE AND PROCESS: Instead of writing your vision statement again here, take these words into the world with you. Decide how you will note the vision, making it so plain you could view it on the run. Hold these words as a mantra to your movement, theming this dream life you are actively creating.

CHAPTER 6
OUTCOMES

The thing you desire most is that which you control the least.

Heartbreaking, isn't it? I see an agonizing example of this in my hometown of Houston, TX. City planners are constantly designing new and innovative attractions as our city hosts major events, from Final Fours to Super Bowls to World Cup matches.

Ultimately, an ominous truth looms over the region despite the renovations. Every once in a while, a hurricane hits Houston. It's an inescapable fact of fate. Living on the Gulf Coast means you hold a heightened awareness every summer, hoping this won't be the year it happens again. Structures get destroyed, and taxpayer-funded beautification projects get sidelined. This is to say nothing of the bigger disaster, as countless locals suffer displacement and some tragically lose their lives. A space being outfitted to draw in tourists, ironically and inevitably, also sees the day it is evacuated.

Outcomes are fickle like that. We strive toward a planned end, holding a goal in our minds and determination in our hearts, locked in for whatever pieces of the process are up to us. We must also learn to accept it when factors outside our control dash our desires. The world-class athlete who was bound to be named MVP snaps an ACL midseason. The epic road trip comes to a rumbling halt with a flat tire. The dream job announces layoffs.

Why then should we even focus on outcomes? Why even put ourselves in the emotionally vulnerable position of caring? We care because it deepens our character. The boldness it takes to sprint when you can't see the finish line shapes you into the type of person that poet Rudyard Kipling would describe as having an "unconquerable soul." Forged by fire, suffering setbacks, and continually coming back for more makes it so that, over time, it would take a lot more to kill us.

There's a reason that burpees, which require no equipment and can be done at home without a gym membership, are so often featured as programmed movements in gyms. There is nothing harder for us or better for us than falling down and getting back up. To live a life of purpose, we have to fix our relationship to outcomes. We have to accept when life knocks us down and choose to do a burpee. Imagine it as looking as though you've fallen flat on your face, only to then showcase your next move: a powerful upward thrust not only to your feet but also to greater heights as you spring into an emphatic jump. You've inserted energy when it looked like you were spent.

This is what resilience against outcomes looks like. We apply for jobs after being fired. We dare to love again after divorce. We recover from injury and return to practice. Though we determine our course in the beginning and encounter many damning false endings, ultimately, we hold the final say as to what chapters of the story still lie ahead. Regardless of outcomes, it doesn't end until you put down the pen. Let's keep writing a story worth telling.

As a kid, I was pretty good at golf. It wasn't my game of choice, but my dad was as skilled as they come. Never forcing and always inviting, he'd welcome me to join him on the course. While I wasn't necessarily drawn to the sport, I loved being outdoors. I loved the tall trees, the water features off the fairway, and the occasional snow cone. I loved the distinct sound of a nice, crisp tee shot. I loved the science of angles, distance, and backspin. I loved watching Terry Sr. smoke his work buddies and frat brothers with ease, and I felt special getting to ride with the big guys in the cart. I loved the quality time. I loved every minute I spent with Dad.

Eventually, I began to love playing the game itself. This would progress into the old man buying me a set of clubs and hiring a golf instructor. This is where the invitation began to meld with expectation. An investment in my development was being made. What would I do with it?

I did what any kid growing up in the Clutch City era would... I gave 100 percent of my attention to our beloved, back-to-back World Champion Houston Rockets and resolved to hoop. I, too, was going to hoist the coveted Larry O'Brien trophy someday, and nobody could convince me otherwise. Besides, what kid in their right mind would choose a polo and slacks over the fad for oversized AND1 shorts with the matching headband?

I went off the deep end, collecting trick-shot VHS tapes and seeking acceptance from a whole new friend group, immersing myself in an entirely new identity sequence. Thinking back, I don't believe it to be defiance. I feel this was my first big act of independence. I'd made a decision about how I wanted to show up in the world, and I was clear on my desired outcome. I'd grow up and win an NBA title.

There came a day when my dad was invited to play in the Shell Houston Open pro-am event. He'd asked me to come along and be his caddy. The experience was unreal. We got to stand mere feet away from some of the best in the game, and I would walk the course with him as he knifed his way through a masterful round with long drives, pristine command of the irons, and rangy putts.

He challenged me that day, expressing that while he'd support me no matter what sport I chose, golf would be the best route to a scholarship. This would be the game I could play beyond the age of sixty. If I ever wanted to play at an elite level, this was my lane. "When you get older, you'll remember this conversation," he said. A former dual-sport athlete himself, having broken his high school's basketball scoring record and being quite a slugger in baseball too, he reminded me that our family doesn't grow taller than average. He questioned whether I had a future in hoops but then showed up faithfully to support me at every game he could.

Fast-forward: I have never taken golf seriously again. To this day, my mind understands good golf through the priceless exposure in my formative years, but my body cannot produce it after decades of separation. I can smoke heads at a friendly trip to Top Golf while enjoying buffalo wings between my turns, but on a course, I live in the sand, the woods, and the water.

Indeed, as an adult now, I remember that conversation with my dad. He was right. I would've had better prospects in what I was invited into than in what I'd chosen for myself. He didn't have his golf legacy carried forward by his only son. Basketball did not work out for me, at least as a player. This was the outcome.

The good news is that it doesn't end with outcomes. Consider the *impact.*

Though I didn't become a golf pro, my old man had a tremendous impact on my development in sports, leadership, and the practice of fundamentals essential to human flourishing. I became obsessed with the sports performance process, earning a master's degree in human performance, launching a coaching brand, and facilitating strength and conditioning programs for many professional athletes, including golfers.

As I write this, I am closing in on my fortieth birthday, still competing in the pro division of a hybrid fitness racing series, my current sport of choice. And as for basketball? Humbly, the 5'9" guy who had no shot at impacting the game as a player has found a lane to the ball. I've been blessed to serve the Boston Celtics over the past four seasons in a consulting capacity, providing mindset and organizational coaching for players, coaches, and executives. I got to play a small part in a big thing, supporting the team during the historic run that would see an eighteenth banner raised, cementing the organization's distinction of holding the most world championships in basketball history.

As a fun wrinkle to this plot, one of the coaches in Boston was a player in Houston during my childhood and a big part of the Clutch City squad, yet another reminder that the seed of vision planted in the head of a toddler leads to the harvest of virtue later, emerging in the heart of a leader.

Wild, isn't it? I needed the desired outcome to enter the space I was purposed to occupy, only for God to allow things that looked like failure and disappointed my support system to ultimately guide me to my unique angle of impact. I found a way to that Larry O'Brien trophy, inconceivably far from my planned path.

It bears noting that we sometimes see failed outcomes playing out to a positive end. We can celebrate being wrong when the impact shows up right. Consider the loblolly pine, a tree named after mud. This tree is unique to the Southeastern U.S., and in fact, its presence comprises the largest forest in the country. Sprawling across 14 states and covering over 29 million acres, it cannot be held within the confines of a designated national forest area. People live and work among the loblollies, coexisting with them. There are no planned vacations to see the pines because their ubiquitous presence is the standard backdrop to neighborhoods, Little League fields, and highway commutes. They're so abundant, we take their majesty for granted.

This tree was first called "loblolly" by British explorers who found it to only grow in marshy areas with mud the texture of stew. The derogatory nickname stuck, as people in the lumber trade believed it would never have commercial value or be able to grow anywhere but the swamps. This tree was relegated to the mud, and the understood outcome was that they'd have to find another resource to build communities.

The true outcome? Because most tree seedlings cannot grow in the conditions this pine needs, it had no competition for germination space. The loblolly seed found gold in the garbage, embracing mud as a premium self-moisturizing soil, and it began to reproduce and tower magnificently over every area it inhabited. Maturing to heights greater than 110 feet in some places, the loblolly pine is the single tallest natural structure in every geographic zone in which it grows. To be sure, they've even found their way to some mountaintops, setting roots in rare pockets of humid subtropical mire to cement their crown at the peak.

To the consternation of early experts, this tree has become the single most commercially significant of its kind, now used for construction, furniture, and paper. There is a high probability that something sharing space with you right now in the room you're in was crafted from a loblolly pine. The studs providing a skeletal structure to your home were likely built from the wood of this pine. When you find yourself sitting at a wooden table, consider that a vast percentage of these, too, are crafted from this tree. The page you are reading right now may have been made from one of them.

The loblolly shows us that even what is discounted and disrespected can thrive. It's not only that we can have our dreams dashed when we hope for the good and see an outcome of underperformance. Sometimes, we underestimate a thing and get ironically rewarded as our planned outcome gets outperformed. What could the "experts" know of this treasure of a tree, after all, considering that we now know its DNA sequence is greater than seven times more complex than that of a human? We never stood a chance at calling the outcome, and now we find ourselves stunned, awestruck in gratitude for its impact. Outcomes can outshine predictions. The thing we've relegated to the mud in our lives can become the highest rising feature and most valuable resource.

Shockers happen. The 2007 New England Patriots became the first team in history to go undefeated through the entirety of the 16-game regular season, then continued their run of terror without blemish through the playoffs, looking untouchable as they arrived unbeaten at the Super Bowl. That night, they would lose the only game of the season that held any historical significance, bested by the New York Giants, who, just one year prior, were a middling team with as many losses on their record as wins.

The outcome? A failure at locking up history. But the impact? A young Patrick Mahomes would later tell the story of watching this game at age twelve and being inspired to chase a dream. He now holds three rings of his own, with former Patriots great Tom Brady calling his games as a journalist and openly acknowledging his greatness.

Were Brady's Pats any less great for this loss, when they amassed seven other titles in the biggest legacy run their sport has seen? And what if young Patrick hadn't been inspired by the game that sealed his love for football? Perhaps he would've stuck to baseball, and the Chiefs' dynasty would've never emerged. And how about those Giants? They'd long underwhelmed any expectation tied to their name, showing up small. Their legacy took a turn when they ousted the expected outcome and created instant impact.

I've known shocking wins and devastating losses. My wife and I recently put a business to bed in the most painful of ways. We'd seen the glory days, when revenue flowed freely, media sources published stories on our life's work, and notable celebrities would even pop into our gyms for a good sweat. We'd been blessed to even enjoy some agility, investing in and launching other businesses. We'd transitioned one business on our own terms, feeling no material impact. We'd sold our shares in a restaurant we co-owned, drawing a profitable exit even during the pandemic. We'd sold another business and seen financial gain from it.

But the mothership, the brand tied to our faces, our social recognition, and our legacy up to that point, was trending downward and ready to be put to sleep. To be clear and mince no words, it failed. There came a grim day when we had to deliver tragic news to our investors, partners, team, and clientele, with no blaming of the economy, the competition, or the multitude of external factors beyond our control. This was our outcome. We'd tried our best, and now we owned our loss.

When I think back on the impact of our gym brand, however, I see all the things that don't fit into a spreadsheet and can't be accounted for on a profit-and-loss statement. There was the person who informed us that in their rock-bottom moment, battling with suicidal ideation, a mindset coaching moment during a workout inspired them to stay alive. Another reported that the gym was the only place in their life in which they felt strong, and it empowered them to leave an abusive relationship. There was a client and friend who'd fallen on hard times, whom we discreetly allowed to live out of the office space for a season.

Many reported symptoms reversing, healing from chronic disease, and achieving the dream-come-true moment of no longer being bound to medications. Then there were the people who'd met up for a class on a first date, as it meant a safe place to connect over a shared interest, ultimately leading to me officiating their weddings, one of them taking place right there *in the gym*. People who had met through our movement were then having babies. Literally, humans came into being because this brand was present. I am in awe of what that twelve-year journey brought into the world.

Again, to be clear. A failure must be called what it is. There is no "but," though I would argue there is an "and." Nobody goes undefeated. Nothing lives forever, and during the finite time a pursuit is underway, its impact is unique for all time. The world should be forever marked by the movement, long after the sun sets on its final day. A thing that has saved troubled lives and started new ones is, by definition, life-changing. Regardless of the outcome, this is its *impact.*

Honoring impact is not a cheap tactic of mental gymnastics to avoid the pain of loss, but rather a reminder, like AND1 hoop shorts and trick-shot VHS tapes, that a dream is worth pursuing, even if it doesn't ultimately lead to the desired destination. It wasn't truly a destination you were chasing in the first place, but rather a destiny. It was always about what discipline you would honor, what masterpiece you would design, and who you would become in the process.

Getting clear on a desired outcome is key to setting a goal. Your purpose depends on it. Releasing attachment to the outcome means you welcome any path to your eventual win, unlocking an appreciation for the impact you'll have on the world.

So, hold to your outcomes lightly and to your impact tightly. Dare to chase not only direction but also destiny. The most important outcome is that you *outlast* and *overcome.*

PAUSE AND PROCESS: What's your big goal? After getting clear on that, unpack it. What underlying impact is made possible by this goal, regardless of outcomes?

PART TWO
CHOOSING GROWTH

After becoming clear on your life's purpose using the ENVIVO method, it's time to work on developing a growth-oriented mindset. If purpose is the below-ground chasm we dig to lay a firm foundation, growth, then, is the rising tower of bricks we build from the ground up. Notice what we're doing here. We've established a means by which we will support all we're about to explore next, allowing it to stand secure against storms well into the future.

A fixed mindset is the default setting of the human brain. With a fixed mindset, we believe our circumstances are our ceiling. This means we believe that what we have now is all we will get. We are convinced that bad news is final and that a "no" is not short for "not yet." The untrained human brain will usually accept failure not only as an event but also as an identity.

A fixed mindset isn't inherently bad or wrong; it's a sign that our neurocircuitry is working correctly. The brain protects the body. It's instinctual and makes logical sense. Because your thoughts keep you from venturing beyond pain or disappointment, you can safely choose to mitigate risk and fall back. But as we know from the old clichés we hear ad nauseam, ships safely docked at the shore are not living out their purpose, and smooth seas have never made skilled sailors. We've got work to do in shifting from a fixed mindset to a growth mindset.

With a growth mindset, we believe our circumstances are merely information connected to opportunity. This means that we take in negative perception inputs, like fear, rejection, and even physical pain, and calmly run them through a filter, taking personal autonomy to decide for ourselves whether what we are experiencing is a wall we've run into or a speed bump we can roll past. With this mindset, we can absorb risk, defy the odds, wake the dog in us, and push beyond comfort to unlock new levels of awareness and capability. It takes some courage and a lot of practice to adopt this mindset.

A common expression in the neuroscience world is, "Neurons that fire together, wire together." This means that the more often we direct our brain to follow a new pattern through our decisions and actions, the more it begins to prefer this new pattern as its default. Sound familiar? We explored this a bit in the earlier study of habit formation as it pertains to visioning, and it applies here, too. It's quite powerful, actually, how much seeking purpose and choosing growth are genuinely connected, even at the level of the brain.

Based on my extensive work in personal growth and my research background, I find that a growth mindset comprises four ingredients. These superpowers are not a linear list, and you don't need to graduate from one to gain access to the next. These four virtues will help you soften what appears hard, find the fortitude to fight for your desired outcome despite obstacles, hold sincerest appreciation for the struggle and extract joy from it, and then look back on a mission conquered or survived with a rewarding sense that you've learned and grown.

These are our four pillars of growth mindset:

- **Grace:** Forgiving people and circumstances, including yourself, that have led to your suffering.
- **Grit:** Stone-cold work, built on belief. The ability to lean into the hard thing that leads to the good thing.
- **Gratitude:** Welcoming abundant joy in the present moment and task, reframing a burden as a blessing.
- **Growth:** Channeling the above virtues to access new levels of awareness and ability. Forging the self.

Carrying your ENVIVO learnings intentionally, it's now time to advance. In section two, you will learn how to grow through what you go through. As a fair warning, this will cost you. It's an invitation to notice and dismiss ego, welcome humility, and prepare to be amazed at what exuberant pleasure you can find in the things you once thought were too hard to crack. Enjoy the journey.

CHAPTER 7
GRACE

The difference between a flower and a weed is judgment.

Our family has a morning practice. It goes unspoken and unbroken. Without anyone delegating the task or checking a clock to be reminded that it's time to turn the knobs, this simple daily rhythm is regularly enacted at dawn, cued by a natural event, and refreshes us all with a sense of connection to the world outside our home. As the sun rises, we open the blinds and turn off any lights. Our home has large windows that invite natural light in, and we welcome it at the break of each new day, enjoying breakfast unplugged. The light of a rising sun graces the table as our littles eat their breakfast. There's something about it that settles our nervous systems, rejuvenates our spirits, and primes our mood for the day ahead.

One particularly hectic morning, as we mediated trivial sibling spats, distributed morning vitamins, and ensured everyone had their socks on, a sudden and stunning pause of peace fell over our home. As my wife opened the blinds, she noticed that the most vibrant magenta flowers had come into bloom and were now greeting us in a gorgeous display at first light. She called the kids over to the window, pointing out the pretty petals, which even I have to admit were charming to behold.

For a moment, the kids forgot about the toy they'd bickered over. Mommy's mind was at ease while she took in the delight. I sidelined all commentary about our need to hurry so we could make it out of the door for school on time. We all simply paused, taking a moment to enjoy the view.

My mind (the seat of emotion, belief, consciousness, and will) enjoyed the simple beauty and the sweet moment it brought us. My brain (the analytical organ in my head) opened a new tab, noting on my to-do list that I'd need to have a second look at these beautiful buds after returning from school drop-off. Upon further investigation, my awe shifted to obligation. Nothing haunts a "yard dad" with an anxiety-inducing primal call to duty like what I'd just realized. These pretty little pods dancing in the breeze were, in fact, weeds. Not on my watch.

After giving myself a little grace for missing the seasonal calendar update that pings me to lay organic pre-emergent weed treatment, I got to work. The pretty flowers had an ugly story. They were part of a plant called the musk thistle, a noxious and invasive rascal that found its way to Texas grasslands in 1852 after a seed-mixing incident. This baddie spreads rapidly wherever it takes root, with each plant producing upward of 20,000 seeds, all prone to becoming airborne and launching a takeover of any yard or prairie they touch.

Once the thistle enters the rosette stage, herbicides fail to get the job done. And how do we know we've graduated to that phase? You guessed it: flowering. Further compounding matters, its stem body is fibrous, thorny, and sticky, making it unfriendly to the plucking hand. This would be an unpleasant job. I'd need to get to the root and manually remove them. It was time to eradicate the intruder.

I've learned that lawn work is a lot like life work. If left unchecked, unhealthy things can set strong roots in our lives. We can't just go wrestle an unwanted thing away because there are thorns to consider. We've got to treat the unwanted thing almost as if we adore it. We have to forgive its pesky presence, allow ourselves to get intimately close to it, and take great care to gently unearth it. Chopping heads off the beasts only allows their seeds to scatter more rampantly. Even an honest attempt to pull out roots, if not done with careful completeness, leaves landmines of potential regrowth festering beneath the surface of the lawn. In many cases, you've got to soak and soften the soil, then go in with a shovel, scooping well below the root line, and lift the unwelcome visitor like a delicate gem before mindfully moving it to a bin without risking a fumble.

Then comes the truth that you now have craters. Like tombstones, these obvious reminders memorialize the fact that something dead was dealt with here. The lawn would've ironically been a better candidate for yard of the month with the weeds than it is now with these deep divots. There's also the reality that grass won't just naturally regrow and level off in these areas. You've now got the job of laying new soil, aerating it (a process of puncturing holes in the ground, allowing oxygen to enter the soil), and then laying new grass seed. The new seed will need to be kept moist for ten days straight for the grass seed to germinate, a tall task in the high-heat Texas climate. This means a lot of watering.

Grace works the same way. We've got to honor what shows up as dishonorable, memorializing the menacing pieces we wish had never entered our lives. To carry all of our purpose work into the formation of a renewed mindset, we must not "just let things go," but rather process, reframe, and patiently and actively heal from them. We've got to do two hard jobs: pull a weed and sow a seed.

The goal is growth, and growth relies on grit. Grit will take you deep into the trenches, leveraging every heavy-duty task that gets the job done. This often means discovering a new kind of wonder akin to gratitude and then giving the circumstance your grace. Was I grateful for the weeds? No. Was I grateful for what I learned in the process of gracefully removing them? Absolutely.

On a lighter note, not all weeds are perpetually invasive, and some you can choose to live with. Again, lawn work reflects life work. Not every annoying person is a person you cut off. Some are assigned to teach you tolerance.

I was once invited to an NFL game by a restaurant chain that our gym had partnered with. It was fun! I'd run in a race across the end zone at halftime, stacking props to "build a burger." Because the stakes included a grand-prize gift card if I won, and the prospect of public humiliation before a sold-out crowd if I lost, I did not show much grace to my opponent. Even in a fuzzy bun-shaped suit that impeded my strides, I was cookin' with speed. The crowd actually got far more engaged than I thought was possible for these awkward sideshow spectacles that happen during TV breaks.

After the win, I was soon given the chance to put on my grace face. A surly man, appearing to be a few beers in and spilling his current one carelessly, hurled criticisms in the media tunnel upon my exit from the field: "I thought for a coach you'd be faster than that.

Gotta work on your cardio, bro. You're lucky they didn't put you out there with somebody in your own line of work."

In hindsight, all of this is so silly. I'm too big a person to be engaged in that smallness, right? I'd like to imagine I'm the type of saint who just brushes off the b.s. and walks away. But in that moment, fueled by adrenaline and probably a bit of arrogance, too, I was unsober on zero beers. I felt the intoxicating urge to say something I'd later regret. I almost matched his energy at the risk of escalation, but then I quickly caught myself, reminded by my convictions that doing right quietly holds more value than sounding right loudly. Besides, I wanted to be invited back. Why ruin it?

When I later redeemed that gift card, I held a mindful moment about this encounter over a good meal. I recalled a quote attributed to Babe Ruth: "The loudest boos come from the cheapest seats." Ain't that the truth? The person not invited to participate stands on untested ground, berating the man in the arena.

Applying that same logic, we can zoom out. Somebody hundreds of feet above me, far from the field, whose voice I couldn't have heard, probably said much worse about me at no risk of drawing a response. There's also the truth that I am no NFL athlete. I was a man in a fuzzy suit, playing a goofy game; any hater I ran into wasn't the worst of them, just the one in my face. How could I have ever taken offense to this foolery? I'm glad I made the decision not to trifle in the tunnel. This was a weed to leave be.

Some weeds we let live because they bring a harmless charm. Dandelions are weeds. My generation grew up calling them flowers and making a childhood game of blowing their domed fragments into the wind, having no care for the fact that we were spreading a frickin' pest. But hey, though they are an irritant to lawns, they have holistic and diuretic benefits for humans.

This is kind of like the idea that not everyone who calls you out is a hater. Sometimes, they're honest, but accountability feels like an attack when you're not open to growth. Wait. Am I preaching to myself here? Maybe I *was* slow in that burger suit and should just own it without defense. We can let some annoyances remain rooted, as they may do more for the development of our souls than the disturbance of our soil. Those famous clovers we call good luck? Yep. They're weeds, too. Get this: even the universally beloved daisy is, by agricultural definition, a weed.

To transition from a fixed mindset (my circumstances are my ceiling) to a growth mindset (my circumstances are information connected to opportunity), we've got to practice grace daily. Whether or not we choose elimination, sometimes, you've just got to call a weed a weed. This isn't the most popular definition of grace, but let's wrestle with this thought...

Sometimes, grace means just calling a thing what it is and letting it be exactly that. When we don't pathologize a thing to the positive, or crop, filter, and caption it to make it more socially savvy and digitally digestible, we can feel freedom in wisdom. We now know and can freely declare that we aren't blinded by weeds, naively crowning them as flowers.

Giving grace to people and circumstances grants us freedom. Reflecting on the neutral mindset portion of our ENVIVO framework, it's essential that we do the work of learning to forgive everyone or anything that has contributed to our emotional maladies. This can be hard, but it medicates our emotional state, allowing us to show up as people who have carried wounds and seen them turn to scars.

We can still carry reminders that they were wounds and simultaneously acknowledge that they no longer bleed. Sometimes, this takes therapy or deep inner work. It's not to be taken lightly, nor is anything written here intended to trivialize your trauma. We can spend an entire life working to get past things, and some of them may still follow us to the grave. Life's imperfect like that, and for this, you can give yourself grace, too.

Grace is one of those things that helps the floodwaters recede, such that our thoughts and feelings can escape emotional hijack and complete the trek to logic and reason. Grace turns down the boil and buffers off the steam so we can see ourselves clearly again, reflecting a pleasant presence off a calm and clear surface.

When will you give yourself grace?

Imposter syndrome. The inner critic. The intrusive thought that whispers, *You are not enough.* The incomprehensible error you've made. The indefensible injustice you committed hurt people and now hurts you, even as a thing of the past. These are all examples of weeds in your mind. They won't lead you to a lush life and vibrant fullness. Lying to yourself about their identity cannot help the grass grow greener.

Forgive yourself, and in so doing, free yourself. Allow yourself to no longer show up smelling like your situation. Make room not to be halted at the age of error, but emboldened by the wisdom you've gained from the soaking, digging, extracting, and replacing. Aerate your mind and sow new seeds. Put on a new identity and square your shoulders to face yourself in the mirror, calling what you see there "good."

Remember, when we pull a weed, we sow a seed. In this context, where the weed is judgment, the seed is compassion. May your life and your lawn be lush.

Ever the two-edged sword, we must also resolve not to abuse grace. It's not enough to simply acknowledge it. We must appreciate it. There is a difference. The person who over-indexes on the celebration of grace certainly acknowledges its presence, yet finds themselves curiously landing in more and more circumstances that would require grace from others. Believing in its abundance as a resource, and knowing that in its purest, God-given form, it will never run out; they may allow themselves to be poisoned by pride and commit repeated offenses of the same kind.

Avoid this path.

While one lawn owner passively pays a landscaper to handle the weeds and never thinks twice about the habits that help them thrive, another knows the laborious toil of removing these beasts and resolves to suffocate any chance of resurgence.

Grace can be wielded in the same way. This applies to the person who has had to admit a tragic mistake, who has been publicly disgraced but then embarrassingly owned the error, or who exposed themselves by coming clean before they were caught. A person who has journeyed perilously into the desperate need for grace and miraculously received it forms a deeper appreciation of it, sparking seeds of gratitude that yield a harvest of new patterns.

Treat others with the same grace *you* need. Hold yourself just as lightly. Sometimes, you've got to remove and replace. Other times, you choose to allow the presence of something that can be both a friend and a foe. Still other times, you just call it like you see it and allow that to be empowering in itself. Remaining in an open headspace of curiosity, you'll know when and how to use each of these tools when the time is right.

Just remember, the difference between a flower and a weed is judgment.

Our journey in growth begins when we embrace the gift of grace. This isn't just a cheap trick to make you feel better; it's a clearing of the slate, removing the power of any person or circumstance to cloud your mind. Grace brings freedom. With a renewed mind, the fog clears, and you are able to access the tools of grit and gratitude, leading to growth.

PAUSE AND PROCESS: Where in your life have you called a weed a flower? Should this weed be removed and replaced? Might it be healthier for it to remain present? How might you develop the ability to call it like it is? Lastly, how will you work to replace judgment with compassion in how you view yourself, and what will this make possible in your life?

CHAPTER 8
GRIT

Enroll, then engage.

The bison's entire life is themed by work. The beast of the prairie seems not to mind it and even finds joy and fulfillment in it. This has contributed to the species' longevity, as it has been around for more than 300,000 years and has repeatedly adapted to new environmental demands. Era by era, bison have chosen the hard way and proven it was the only way. Their survival against brutal circumstances shows us that shortcuts may look smart but are ultimately not wise.

There *is* a difference between smart and wise. Bison operate in a simple two-part mental map: problem and solution. They count the cost and resolve to pay it, getting the job done. This plays out in mind-blowing displays of strength, endurance, and organizational prowess.

If there's an individual threat, even if woken from slumber and not in peak readiness, the bison chooses to fight. If there's a communal threat, the bulls arrange themselves in a large circle, welcoming an inner circle of their female partners and then an innermost circle of their young, providing a bold barrier of protection against any intruder and reinforcing for themselves that social safety is the standard.

If there's a trek to be had for vital resources, such as food, the bison will literally use their neck, shoulders, and forehead as a snowplow, plodding through dense tundra up to six feet deep, covering as many as 70 miles of hiking in a single season.

Long story short, this breed finds a way. They do not sit idly by, negotiating with themselves, consulting their feelings, or accepting a regression in means. They figure it out. They get it done.

Perhaps the most fascinating display of situational grit is their response to the prospect of oncoming inclement weather. Bison know intuitively that to run away from a storm would only lead to being caught up in it later and therefore being under its severe onslaught for a longer and more perilous period.

Thus, they operate in a paradox of poise. Calmly and communally, they walk together into the storm. Taking on the affront headfirst means that they are not surprised or flustered by the dangers ahead. They embrace fate, relinquish what they cannot control, and boldly commit. In doing so, they choose a path toward sunshine. Though they get hit hard, they soon emerge on the other side, with the threat behind them.

Imagine that: a life where one sees more sun by chasing more storms. Grit pays dividends, increasing the quality of life. By contrast, cattle notoriously run from storms, and sadly, this has led to cases of them being taken for a ride in tornadoes. That can't end well.

Point taken. Be the bison. Lean into the hard thing that leads to the good thing.

In the research leading to psychologist Angela Duckworth's best-selling book, aptly titled *Grit*, she discovered that the combination of passion and perseverance over a sustained time horizon is the single strongest predictor of future success. The groundbreaking discovery made it clear that grit beats smarts, good looks, and even physical health, making it our best means of achieving goals and advancing. Those who work with people in developmental or competitive spaces can attest to seeing this play out consistently.

I was once invited to serve as a guest speaker at a prominent Division I NCAA football program. Being a fly on the wall before my speech afforded me a masterclass I'll never forget, as I got to see firsthand how the best leaders in the world muster grit within their fold. The head coach was closing spring training camp, issuing an unremarkable, painstakingly blunt edict to the team about their preparation for summer practice. Nothing he said was profound, yet everything he said was pointed.

"Men, good job this spring. We've got a lot to work on, but we've got an opportunity to put in that work. You'll now have a couple of weeks off." He scanned the room in silence, first calmly, then more intensely. Making direct eye contact with many of the players, he made certain the pause brought a healthy measure of urgency and discomfort.

Then he became stern and continued (this time with higher volume and lower regard for feelings): "How you spend this time is on you. Eat snacks and play patty cake on the phone with your ex if you want to, but on June 6th, you will show up, and so will the work. Year over year, the heat index on that date averages 104 degrees. The heat will hit you in the face like a shovel, and he don't care." He personified the heat, conjuring mental imagery of it showing up as a burly adversary, wielding a weapon with no regard for anyone's feelings. Ouch.

He was making it clear: the conditions would not be friendly, and the work would be mandatory. These men would now need to independently manage their time with accountability in mind. Soon, it would be time to show up like a herd of bison, embracing the storm and finding a sense of foolish joy in the grit, charging forward into the onslaught, believing firmly that they'd see fulfillment on the other side. If they wanted to keep their position on the roster and contribute to the team's winning, they'd have to go all in on the hard way.

It works the same way for you and me outside of the sporting context. The work is the work. There is no way around the work. While we have freedom of choice in how we manage our time and leisure, there will come a definitive date when the work greets us unkindly. He who forsakes the work, the work shall expose.

We see in these examples that grit is simple and also that simple is not easy. The hard, unsexy work without fanfare or validation is not complicated. There is no rocket science to showing up. You either do or do not commit to and conquer the quest. The grit equation, laid bare, is as follows.

Enroll, then engage.

This means that we sign up, and then we *show up*. We commit to the work, and then we simply do the work. We get clear on the problem, and without softening it in our minds or looking for somewhere to hide and someone to blame, we go all in on pursuing the solution.

This can be particularly challenging if what we are being enrolled in is not by choice. For example, maybe your job has let you go, and the rent is due. Your spouse has chosen to leave, and you've got kids to raise. You've endured a terrible injury or received a devastating medical diagnosis. Grit is an unkind call to embrace the bitter truth that sometimes even what is not your fault is now your responsibility. Like the bison, you can't choose to sit out the trek because sustenance is on the other side of the storm. Like the team, you can't afford to trifle in fun, because camp is coming, and glory awaits on the other side of the grind.

When life deals us an unfair hand, we can absorb a loss or fight for a win. Grit is what empowers one through a daunting job search, a brave quest in single parenting, or a long road in rehab. Without downplaying our sadness, we can choose to endeavor toward our gladness. Own it, face it, and shift it. When the mind is made up, the nervous system aligns. The muscular system readies itself for load, and a biological cocktail of passion and perseverance is embedded in every fiber of our being.

The adult human body is composed of an estimated 37 trillion cells, all of which are seated in an auditorium, eagerly awaiting instructions on what to believe. Your thoughts are the coach here. When the head is committed, the heart follows. Here's the kicker: The fact that you even picked up this book on purpose and the growth mindset it reflects suggest that you are the type of person who wants to reframe your thought life in a way that drives freedom and success.

Everyone would grow in grit if the work came without hindrance, but that's a fairy tale. Each of us has barriers in our way and a need to remove them to unearth opportunities. Consider the players in the earlier example. Despite already having skills and a strong work ethic, and having been highly recruited for good reason, the law of averages suggests that a significant percentage of the room felt a perceived gap between their current selves and their best summer-practice selves.

Maybe it was the prospect of the heat making the drills miserable. Maybe it was a subconscious comparison trap, as even gifted athletes know they are being evaluated against one another, and every man is one rep away from being benched or shipped out in the transfer portal.

No matter what is blocking you mentally, it's time to find it and fight it. In the two practices detailed here, we'll work through how to stop your inner critic in its tracks, giving you access to the superpower of grit.

PRACTICE 1: IDENTIFY YOUR BARRIERS TO GRIT

The first and most crucial step in unlocking grit is identifying what's blocking your path to it. In a sense, you're finding your mind's weakest link so you can then coach it up. Barriers to grit may include things that don't feel good to realize or admit about yourself, but sit in solitude and note these things.

With self-compassion and no self-judgment, mindfully record a short list of what stands between you and the work. Things that make the list may include "fear of failure," "feeling unprepared," "impostor syndrome," or even the classic "laziness."

As a next step, I challenge you to ask someone else to share with you what they see as a barrier to your grit. But don't ask just anyone. This needs to be someone who knows you at an intimate level and will be honest with you, like a trusted family member, romantic partner, or long-time best friend.

I think of it like this: I have a mirror in my bedroom that somehow casts a leaner reflection and also a mirror in my bathroom that's brutally honest. It's probably just due to light and angles affecting how the image is cast. Not that I spend too long in front of mirrors, but I have noticed this, and I appreciate it. I want the report I receive to be free of flattery, so I often intentionally choose the honest mirror. The person you select for this needs to be exactly that: an honest mirror. You want someone who can see you clearly and tell you truthfully what they notice as a limit in your life. This brings the gift of clarity.

Once you've compiled your list and then added a barrier from an honest mirror, take fifteen minutes to be with it. Write about a barrier freely, holding it close and calling it what it is, without mincing words. Speak to the ways it has held you back and the impact it has had on your ability to honor the work in front of you. Your barriers will be hard to tame until you are willing to give them a big hug. Daring to come into close contact and embracing things, as your brain tells you there's no longer a need to subconsciously battle them, allows you to make peace with them so they don't fight you as hard when you respond to them.

For some, it's as simple as time management. You don't wake up on time. You don't manage your waking hours well. You don't sleep enough, so you're sluggish in returning to work the next day. For others, it's the classic thought traps. You're too negative and can't rise above the ceiling you've set, or you're passively positive and not taking the wheel, so you're unprepared when life deals you lemons.

Or maybe, like a client of mine, you're navigating a more complex condition. A member of our former fitness family, with whom I did some mindset coaching, discovered that he might be exhibiting some traits of autism. He smiled when sharing this news with me. I was so proud of him, as I could tell this felt like destiny and not doom. He felt like suddenly he had answers for questions he'd long been asking, and life now made more sense. Like a person wearing glasses for the first time, he had found his entire world coming into clear focus. He was able to see now that his life leading up to that point, though it felt normal from the perspective he'd once carried, had room to be honed, sharpened, and refined.

To this day, I love seeing this guy's updates, as he hasn't lost that ear-to-ear grin. He lives out what others have called a problem and carries it as a source of power. Various elements in his life reflect its impact. He has a great career in engineering. He has a special kind of connection with his friends: open and honest, not stuck in small talk. He is finding serious joy in his journey. This is what a reframed barrier looks like.

With the realization that this can be hard for most people and the awareness that we connect best through vulnerability, I want to candidly share that my biggest barrier to grit, for far too long, has been distraction. I don't even mean just losing focus due to outside stimuli; I mean ruining progress from many angles, stifling my ability to do my best work by fooling myself into thinking I was ever even in the work.

For much of my life, like the tread on a tire, I needed traction in the worst way. Action relies on traction. But I was distracted, meaning I was not hitting the pavement, which was killing my chances of moving forward powerfully.

Think about it: distraction = dis-traction.

It's the removal of traction: meaningful frictional contact with the surface upon which action is empowered. I needed to ditch distraction to find traction, sparking action. Make sense? I'll explain.

I believe that my relationship with distraction has been rooted in dopamine addiction. This led me deep into a pit of subconscious self-sabotage. I was absolutely unaware that I was tanking my self-discipline and stifling my chances to achieve my goals.

Dopamine is what neuroscientists call a "happy hormone." It's the chemical our endocrine system releases into our bodies in times of desire and reward. When stewarded diligently, it has incredible use cases. Long, slow projects that eventually lead to progress can elicit a lasting dopamine response. Delaying gratification and eventually solving a complex puzzle can slowly build the joy of desire, then crescendo into a climax of novelty and reward, rooted in newfound confidence upon completion.

Leaning into the work in a way that properly uses dopamine could look like declining to continue dating someone who's shown their true colors, believing that you'll find a secure relationship in the future; sticking with a stock when the market is down, speculating that you'll ride a wave and see future value; or finishing a degree you've started after enduring some hard courses.

But dopamine is a double-edged sword, and I had been toying dangerously with the wrong edge. Chasing cheap dopamine meant

I was constantly mining for quick hits. I chose anything but the work for these momentary hits, meaning I never beheld it in its building but rather abused it in its absorption. I was here to take, take, take, and not to give. I hacked the happy hormones prematurely, duping my brain into believing I'd finished a thing when I'd only finessed a thing. I'd sit out the actual storm but post an inspirational quote on Instagram, inspiring people to enter the storm.

This elicited likes, clicks, follows, and shares, which was rewarding, so I dove deeper down the rabbit hole, choosing the words over the work. I talked too much about my past accomplishments, becoming the person who dines out on old home runs like they can somehow bring new wins. I talked up future goals, too, collecting applause and feeling sky-high on ambition, which, ironically, I couldn't use productively because my brain shut down the desire after the faux reward.

I was too distracted by dreaming. I was too distracted by overthinking. I was too distracted by designing the blueprint to ever build the house. I needed to stop perpetually planning my work and begin actually working my plan. I needed to get quiet in order to love loud. I needed to lock in, mastering time management and diligently slow-cooking the unseen work toward my goals.

Muhammad Ali famously said that no fight is won in the ring, but rather in the many miles on the road and the early mornings in the gym. Stoic philosopher Musonius Rufus pointed out that doing a good thing by hard work means the work passes quickly, but lasting joy remains; yet doing something that looks good without costing you hard work leads to the joy being short-lived, as you then sit in lasting shame.

With the best of intentions and no conscious desire to hurt myself or my team, I was not using my forehead as a snowplow to engage in the cold work of administrative tasks. I was not willing to have my face hit by the shovel that is the heat of showing up well in project management systems. I wanted to sit on the comfortable couch of "Check out this awesome project I've done" in the living room of "Can't you see I'm trying," under the comfy air conditioning of "My last social media post was incredible," while sipping from the coffee mug of "Why do you only point out my losses and not see my wins?"

Mind you, throughout this season of my life, I was a busy and successful person, building brands and leading businesses. People trusted and respected me. I received all the grace you could imagine, as people understood that, as I was only leading them for a short time, I had to cut away many things to focus on the main one. But I knew in my heart that I was forsaking a sacred standard.

It's not only the lazy who lack grit. As an achiever, I genuinely thought I was maximizing my potential, though I was only making use of the tip of the iceberg. After reflecting on my barriers, I now realize that my output could have been significantly greater.

This long, hard look into the brutally honest mirror has helped me to put in long, hard hours doing the *real* work. I am now slowing down to speed up. I am now detail-oriented, patiently approaching tasks and mining for opportunities to optimize, then quickly taking action and attacking them as the mission comes into focus.

Think about how an oven-cooked Thanksgiving meal produces more enjoyment than a microwaved one. My life was already tasty, but this is where I unlocked a whole new world of robust flavor. This is where I found focus, ditching workouts that sounded brutal and impressive on the internet to honor my body with proper stretching and rehab, and doing the slow maintenance miles that ironically make me a faster runner. I traded Wi-Fi for willpower and stories for stamina. I let go of what was holding me back and picked up a whole new self. I've found a way to honor the work I'm up to with a greater sense of joy. I've found a way for the rubber to meet the road, driving traction and taking action.

Let's talk about the *how*.

PRACTICE 2: ELIMINATE YOUR BARRIERS TO GRIT

Now that you're clear on your barriers, it's time to talk back to them. In this practice, we are retraining your brain to bypass what would've previously blocked the road to success.

Remember, neurons that fire together wire together. Over time, as you stack reps and amass experience in choosing the path that leads to who you want to become, your brain will literally begin to form new neural connections that cement your chosen path of thought and action as a new autonomic habit pattern.

This step is vital in your quest toward grit and a growth mindset because we don't get what we want in life; we get what we believe. What we believe is different from what we profess to believe. What we genuinely believe, we embody, and it comes pouring out in our actions. You need traction to achieve action. To get traction, you must hold a firm belief that you can do what needs to be done. Confidence in your competence fuels your courage, and courage gets the work done.

To change your mind and thus change your life, you've got to receive, reframe, and respond.

Kudos to you! By now, you've conquered the first step. And it works like a domino effect: this unlocks the second step, and that second part feeds energy into the third. The more you embrace the process, the more freedom you get out of it.

Receive: Make room to receive the inconvenient realization of your barrier to grit. No matter how big or small it is, give yourself some grace. Allow it, investigate it, and nurture it. It's here, and you now have a means of interacting with it in a life-giving way.

Reframe: Notice what felt like a loss and find a win in it. How can you leverage this perceived weakness to actually show up in strength? Reframing a thought pattern can look like finding specific opportunities to add, remove, or change habits, or like radical acceptance that makes the fight feel like freedom. It could also look like seeking a community of like-minded people so that you have social support as you navigate your interactions with the barrier. Of course, there are also plenty of clinical options if your reframing process is best supported by great resources like therapy.

Respond: Because of the reframe, you can respond rather than react. Where a reaction looks like a knee-jerk clapback that results in defensiveness, denial, or disdain, a response is measured, mindful, and meaningful. Responding looks like quietly wrestling with a thing that feels like a threat, reframing it to allow it to reintroduce itself as a gift, and then confidently expressing gratitude for the learning and a commitment to reciprocal action. This is your path to keeping your cool and making your move.

In fairness, because I shared the story of the hole I was in, it's only right that I share how I climbed out of it. I hope that in my story, you hear a bit of yours, helping you make sense of your thoughts and engage with your limiting beliefs in a way that wakes up the bison in you.

At first, I made every excuse. Again, shame needs somewhere to hide and someone to blame. I always had an eloquent explanation about how I would've and could've done my part if another party had done theirs. This grew tired and played out. I was beginning to see for myself, maybe even before others saw it in me, that I needed to overhaul my systems.

I began to focus on the word "humility." This was the receiving. Viewing life through this lens, I was able to receive alerts on my flaws without rolling my eyes and finding a way out, but instead coming to the realization that I could be elevating myself and everyone around me by making improvements. This was the reframe that turned annoyance into opportunity.

Then, compelled by the reward I knew I could achieve by way of acting on the opportunity, I went big in response. I noticed that my distraction was partly due to insecurity, so I committed to doing the kind of work that fed my confidence, freeing me from having to talk a big game.

I also noticed from conversations with friends who are more successful than me that they spent significantly less time on social media apps. So, I downloaded an app that blocked my socials on an automated recurring schedule, locking up every app I could use to mindlessly scroll, giving me only a small window of access per day, strategically placed in periods outside of work or family time.

I learned in therapy that I was holding on to a lot of regret and operating on a dysregulated nervous system, and I learned in training that I had high levels of cortisol (the stress hormone). So I responded to each element with effort and care, not wishing them away or striving to fix them instantly, but working through every piece of the ENVIVO Method to better understand my path to purpose. I changed my mindset. I slowed down to speed up. I asked more questions, sat with the answers, and emerged as a new me. I found that, in the wake of these new commitments, I was calmer, kinder, and clearer.

Unfazed by the most stressful of days, I was putting in more working hours and also enjoying more leisure time, the good kind, with no glowing rectangle in my hands and lots of tickle time with my kiddos. I had space in my life to dance in the kitchen with my wife. My running and racing were improving as if I were aging backwards. I was showing up sharper for my team and had energy to spare. I brought better ideas to every space I led in and noticed every area of my life falling into a smoother rhythm.

Finally, I was dwelling in confident cadence.

What gets you beyond your barrier? How do you enroll and then engage? Like the bison that receives the realization of a storm, reframes it as an opportunity to chase the sun, and responds by walking forward, what does your personal pursuit of grit look like?

PAUSE AND PROCESS: Name at least one barrier to grit in your life.

____

____

____

____

____

____

____

____

How will you reframe this barrier, and what new opportunity will emerge from it?

____

____

Speaking only in the language of *action*, how will you rise above excuses and reactions in order to mindfully respond? And how will this gritty response unlock a new level of growth for you?

____

____

CHAPTER 9
GRATITUDE

When's the last time you found yourself writhing in joy?

My wife was pregnant for over two weeks past her due date. Whereas a doctor in traditional medicine would've advised a scheduled delivery, our family's trusted holistic doctor shrugged it off, unbothered, welcoming us to consider just allowing our princess to arrive when she was ready.

While I could tell Ashley was growing increasingly uncomfortable, I could also tell she was very attuned to her body's rhythms and accepting of whatever timeline would naturally unfold. She's a warrior, and I fully supported her in the decision. This arrangement made space for us to enter an unexpectedly sweet holding pattern of cancelling or delaying work and family plans. I'd even declined to travel and corner a top-tier UFC athlete I was coaching at the time when a fight got booked near our due date. Not even the most enticing career wins could compare to sitting in the magic of this sacred moment, rife with sweet anticipation. We found ourselves watching the big fight together on TV, laughing about how the baby girl we thought we'd be holding by then was in no hurry to join us.

We had frequent family visits, as many of our next of kin would "just happen to stop by" and hang around the house. The expectancy in the air was so thick that it was palpable. It became a regular occurrence for our parents to be at the house, taking a nap, enjoying an afternoon coffee, or watching our boys, not wanting to miss the birth.

And then, on June 7, 2021, the highly touted day came. Though Ashley had been examined just hours prior and we'd learned that she "likely wouldn't have the baby" that day, as the sun began to set, the telltale signs of active labor began to rise.

Groaning through a lengthy contraction, Ashley asked me to make her a cup of tea. This was not a common ask from her, but I obliged. She didn't take more than a sip of the tea before she felt the urge to go to the bathroom. In another quick turn of events, she didn't complete this task, either, exclaiming that the baby was coming and she feared the birth might happen on the toilet. In the rapid scrum of a twenty-seven-minute active-labor period, baby girl made it clear that just as sure as she'd kept us waiting, she was now ready to make a swift and unforgettable entrance.

With the help of my mother, I laid plastic shower curtains over our bed to mitigate messes. Then Ashley's mom and I toted Ash to the bed. Ashley's father was also present. He contributed in the way that made the most sense to him—he prayed over our family, this baby, and the wild event that was about to transpire. The moment was here. We'd planned a home birth, but not like this. According to our game plan, we'd have our midwife present, an inflated tub of warm water, and even a serene birthing playlist. Nope. No time for pleasantries. It was go time.

I called our midwife, and when she answered, she took on the most soothing tone I've ever heard a human produce. "Dad," she said with astonishingly calm confidence, "I can tell by the sound of Mom's moans in the background that I'm not going to be able to make it to you before the baby arrives. God is with you, and you'll know exactly what to do."

Prior to this experience, I would've told you that this sort of high-pressure, clutch-time scenario creeping up on us is a recipe for being gripped by paralyzing fear. Oddly, though, after spending about five seconds questioning how I felt about the possibility of this leading to a potentially tragic mistake, a whole new engine kicked in. I was primed by faith and intuition, oddly able to understand Ashley's nonverbal cues and to partner with her to bring the miracle from her womb into the room.

As she worked through contractions on her hands and knees, I asked her to scoot forward slightly. We synchronized our breathing and rode the waves of her pain and relief until our beautiful baby girl came forth.

At first, just a head. Had she gotten stuck in the birth canal? Was she choking? How long until the next contraction?? We've got to finish the job! An eerie calm filled the room as we just knew, in a way that we can't explain, that this was going to work out flawlessly. And then it happened. With the ensuing contraction, Rhys, whose name means "vibrant, enthusiastic joy," came tumbling into my arms.

As family helped us to wrap her in towels and Mama worked slowly and intentionally to turn her body, untangling an umbilical cord from around her leg, we had no space in our hearts to be freaked out by the blood splattered on everything, from my shirt to the room's wooden floors. I can only imagine the anguish Ashley felt through the natural, unmedicated birthing process, but doing grueling things with grace and grit is who this warrior of a woman is. She smiled widely as the time had come to hold our daughter tightly to her chest. Ashley is my hero. Rhys is my joy. I grew into a new level of gratitude that day.

When our midwife arrived, so did a few other guests. The midwife's assistant, who'd just frantically left an '80s-themed roller skating party, came sprinting in wearing a neon green tutu over a hot pink leotard with copious amounts of eye shadow and a ponytail flowing to one side out of a massive scrunchy. This whole situation was as comical as her ankle warmers. Way to lighten the mood!

We also had firemen enter, who'd been summoned because Ash lost a lot of blood during delivery. They came thundering in like a military unit, not even realizing the deed had been done. We'd later learn that it's more common than you'd think for firemen to be called in to facilitate births. They had one job that night: to check her blood pressure and confirm her levels were okay. Thankfully, they were, and we were able to send them on their way.

As the crowd parted and our home returned to a more serene space, we gave mom and baby a good bath in healing minerals, had the best conversation with our midwife, and reflected on the unforgettable experience. We shared with her the story of our last date night before the birth, when Ashley had told me that her dream birth would involve just the two of us. Ironically, we had experienced just that. It hadn't been the plan because we valued the guidance, wisdom, and emergency response capabilities of a licensed professional, but as it turned out, we'd lived right into her wildest dream.

What a serendipitous, awe-stricken time of wonder. Her mind, though it had endured shock, agonizing exertion, and the type of work that only producing a body out of a body can put one through, had absolutely no room for dismay. Gratitude shone through her words and her captivating smile. This woman had just weathered a war and yet was being held in a flow of supreme peace. Gratitude is powerful like that.

Dr. P. Murali Doraiswamy, head of biopsychology at Duke University, has uncovered experimental findings showing that if gratitude were bottled up and sold as a drug, it would have an affirmative health-maintenance indication for every major organ in the human body. It can do what even modern medicine cannot. It can bring clarity in calamity and even wellness to your physical systems and cells. There's a reason gratitude is a core component of Alcoholics Anonymous: It's a powerful tool in the process of human healing.

Cultivating the art of thankfulness, then, doesn't just live in your thoughts and bring your mind to ease. It has real-world outputs and can bring life where your impairment brought the threat of death. Even more fascinating, once your mind enters a state of gratitude, it kindly closes the door behind itself, not allowing other thoughts in. You get to fully focus on your life through the lens of welcoming your experience and extracting edifying energy from it.

Meister and Zheng, a student-professor tandem in biological sciences at Cal Tech, published what is perhaps the coolest data on gratitude ever, confirming by research that a brain centered on gratitude becomes a single-track organ. It zeroes in on the joy of the moment, making you impervious to thoughts of doubt and defeat. If harnessed, this becomes another superpower in your arsenal. In this state, you are all gas and no brakes, leaning fully forward into whatever life brings you with confident belief.

Imagine what this can do for you in work, relationships, and your journey in personal development. A no-holds-barred approach to dispensing boundless compassion and holding nothing in judgment. A mind in feral pursuit of pure goodness is not deterred by the occurrence of the contrary. This solidifies what's long been said in an old proverb: "Seeds of bitterness cannot take root in a grateful heart."

Russell Wilson, whose mindset coaching journey we explored in our earlier chapter on neutral thinking, embodies this well. Ever the vocal and emotional leader, he is known to loudly express gratitude in times of trial, using it as a tool to reframe his mind and refine his work. For Russell, gratitude isn't reserved for a quiet moment of peace on the beach in the off-season after it's all worked out; it's a battle cry in the heat of a high-stakes moment. It slows his heart rate and untangles his nervous system. It energizes his spirit. It simultaneously brings his mind into stillness and his body into action.

Hello, flow state. From here, he can operate an elite offense, no matter what defense he faces. When preparing for his first Super Bowl, he reportedly turned his pregame self-talk affirmations into team talk, repeatedly chanting aloud for all to hear, "Gratitude! God is the greatest!" Spoiler alert: he went on to engineer a near-perfect game, beating the Denver Broncos and locking up a championship legacy.

He'd later become a Bronco in a trade, and this mindset persisted there, too. He once tweeted, *"Gratitude... Gratitude, anxiety, and worry can't exist at the same time. Not simultaneously."* Unsurprisingly, this was posted on the heels of a narrow loss, just before a big win to close the season in Denver. Talk about a powerful mindset shift.

Of course, this figure has also seen gut-wrenching losses, too, one of them being in another Super Bowl, one his team should've won at that. A coach made a controversial call, and the quarterback honored his role of submission, releasing elements beyond his control and operating with integrity. The outcome sucked, but not its impact.

He learned a lesson taught for centuries by everyone from Jesus to the Stoics to modern neuroscientists: gratitude will get you through the hardest moments with the softest heart. The farmer shows gratitude even for the rain, knowing in wisdom that the sunshine cannot yield a crop on its own. Bigger than a fuzzy feeling, gratitude is an all-consuming spiritual undertaking, elevating your perspective and transforming you from a "worrier" to a "warrior," undefeated even in an outcome your lower self would call a loss.

What if Russ crumbled after that L? Perhaps he wouldn't have gone on to launch his Why Not You Foundation, centering on health, education, and the alleviation of poverty for at-risk youth, ultimately stacking the kind of wins nobody can take from him, forever changing the lives of many through philanthropic generosity. He now holds a form of recognition even rarer than the coveted Super Bowl ring: the distinction of Walter Payton Man of the Year. This is no team award, and only one person will win it each year, highlighting their gift of winning off the field for the sake of others. Gratitude fuels purpose, passion, and powerful generosity like that.

When's the last time you found yourself writhing in joy? The reference sounds funny at first because we commonly hear the term "writhing" only in association with pain. If we get curious and investigate what the word "writhing" means, it opens up a whole new world for us, one in which we can imagine its application in an entirely opposite scenario.

In its Germanic root, this word refers to a vigorous squirming of the body, which, ironically, is also an automatic physical response to intense celebration. Consider a touchdown dance, the things your body does after finally getting a long-desired positive pregnancy test, or the way you move on a dance floor at your best friend's wedding reception.

In Old English, "writhing" came to refer to a firm fastening of items with rope. In this context, we can take it to mean that it locks something in, unshakably firm. And in the modern English dialect, "writhing" is meant to explain the phenomenon of responding to something you cannot escape or explain, becoming enraptured by a stimulus in your body and fully giving yourself over to it, such that your mind cannot avoid it and your body cannot unfeel it.

Writhing in joy, then, would mean that we have the capacity to get so lost in gratitude, so arrested by joy, so consumed in the highest form of bliss, that we dance and receive. That's it. That's the goal. Dance and receive.

When you feel gratitude welling up, do not fight it. Let it roll through your soul. You don't need actual rhythm or skill to let this life force move through you. You need only to honor the natural cadence of the wave you're riding. Squirm, twist, and pump your fist. High-five a friend. Scream words of thankfulness, whether in front of your team or on a hike where it's heard by nobody but echoed back to you by a rocky amphitheater in resounding fashion. Feel it. Be with it. Allow your mind, body, and spirit to live in the luxury of inhaling gratitude and exhaling grief.

This doesn't just naively shield you from bad thoughts, nor focus you on good thoughts; it drives the whole of your being into clutch mode. Your best decisions are made here. Your perspective is sharpest here. You understand your goals most clearly from this place and are willing to do what it takes to achieve them, regardless of what life throws at you. In the fullness of gratitude, you are unstoppable.

You don't need to be in unmedicated labor or in a championship game to feel this. All you need is present-moment awareness and curiosity. Where the overstimulated and distracted mind scans the world for threats, the open and grounded mind scans the world for thrills.

When you receive kindness from a loved one, don't brush it off or resolve to entertain the sentiment later when life slows down. Receive their wonderful words about you as truth, and welcome them right here in the present moment. This is a gift. Prioritize connection. You'll retire from your work, but you'll never retire from humanity until you take your last breath. Work will help you fund the feeding of your body, but kinship will feed your soul.

When you see a gorgeous sunset, don't glance away to grab your phone. No photo you capture will do it justice anyway. And of all the sunsets in the totality of time, *this one* only happens once. How blessed are you to behold it? Be with it.

When you enjoy a good meal with good people, savor every moment. Eat slowly. Ask a question that challenges the group to reflect and share vulnerably. Consider that this moment of bonding is unraveling your tension and reframing your world view, refreshing you to live as your best self. Allow gratitude to lead you into an investigation of novelty, with one input leading you to mindfully question where you might find another. This is like turning one paycheck into generational wealth by reinvesting it, but it can happen in minutes rather than years, and it's done for your well-being, not your bank account.

For example, if you love the soothing sound of Adele's voice, try letting your streaming app run with the radio function, playing the work of other artists in the same genre. You may discover that under the surface of what was familiar, you become emotionally drawn to the airy delivery of Yebba, spiritually enriched by the pipes of Lauren Daigle, and ushered into a sweet space by the vibes of Naomi Sharon. For everything you're drawn to in familiarity, if you take another look, there is more in store under the surface of the known.

Finding gratitude in small things is closely linked to experiencing awe, a surreal feeling author Sarah Bessey describes as "beholding that which is simultaneously mesmerizing and fleeting." Isn't that something? Being present and curious in a moment helps us see clearly that there is something to honor here and that it's impermanent. We have to be proactive, then, in prioritizing the act of receiving. Even on a hectic day, we must find our pockets of peace. Even in the hustle, it's imperative that we honor the call to harmony.

By the way, I am gladly donating space within the pages of this book to champion one of Sarah's books. *Field Notes for the Wilder-*

ness is a text I will forever feel gratitude for because of the way it's taught me some of the principles I'm sharing with you here. Consider how you might put down your digital device, right next to the anxiety the day has brought on and every other thing that does not serve the best version of you, and become fully alive to the present moment.

Whether it's a high-stakes situation, a run-of-the-mill day in life's busy cadence, or a simple, soft, and sweet moment, notice every opportunity to get curious, widening your perspective on the good and shrinking your sensitivity to the bad. Right now, take a quiet moment to reflect on what gratitude will make possible in your life.

PAUSE AND PROCESS: Where can you shift your mindset toward gratitude? What pain will it help you overcome, and what wins will it unlock in your life?

CHAPTER 10
GROWTH

Grow through what you go through.

All prior chapters have been about information. This one is about integration.

Growth is not something to be pursued, but rather something that ensues. Put simply, when we go all in on understanding our purpose and consciously choose to use grace, grit, and gratitude as tools, especially when we don't feel like it, growth happens.

Let's put the pieces together.

In the pages that follow, you'll take in detailed instructions on how to complete a clarifying guided journaling practice titled *My ENVIVO Growth Chart*. You may flip forward to familiarize yourself with this chart at a glance, but don't fill it out until after first taking in the prompts that precede it.

Many books are read and then forgotten, but this mindfully crafted chart can serve as a compass, reminding you over time of all you've learned and all you're becoming.

These cues organize the practice into simple steps that are easy for the brain to process as the hand writes. You may decide to fill out the chart here in the book, or in a separate journaling space. When finished, consider posting the chart where you'll see it daily, keeping the vision in front of you on your journey forward.

Step 1: Settle into a quiet, undistracted space and play music. Chill vibes only. Instrumental lo-fi, acoustic, smooth jazz, or similar styles work well here.

Step 2: Begin by completing the sentences on the *My ENVIVO Growth Chart* page. In an unhurried manner, reflect on all you took in while reading section one of this book, *Seeking Purpose,* and give your personal responses here. You can repeat responses from the "Pause and process" entries in section one or bring fresh language here. Being brief means you're *clear.* No over-explaining needed; just note what comes up for you in a few words.

Step 3: Now, complete the growth-ingredient prompts in the same manner. On each of the outer dots surrounding the large circle on the graph, write out an element of the ENVIVO method. For example, one will say *"Endeavor,"* another will say *"Neutral Mindset,"* and so on. When finished, you should have all six ENVIVO elements orbiting the large circle. This gives a visual representation of your purpose path, guarding your inner circle. While anything outside of your control remains outside the circle, these pieces are your buffer, defining a space in which you are clear on who you're here to be and can focus on what you're here to do.

Step 4: In each of the large, open spaces within the inner circles (the areas that do not overlap other circles), name an element of the growth ingredients. When this step is completed, the areas of the three inner circles that are not overlapping each other will read *"Grace," "Grit,"* and *"Gratitude."*

Step 5: In the innermost Rouleaux triangle (the point at which all three inner circles converge in the center), write *"Growth."* This is your visual representation that when all elements align, you achieve the goal of growth.

I hope you found this simple exercise helpful. It's the kind of thing I've wished was provided in the many books I've read, helping to galvanize my key takeaways in one place, rather than relying on memory to call forward the information shared over the course of several chapters. As a coach, I wouldn't dare give you tons of passive reading without an accompanying active application assignment, ensuring you have a chance to personalize it, record it, and hold it for future reference and redirection.

When this journaling practice is completed, you will have taken the time to note not only where each piece of this process sits in relation to the others, but you will have also gotten candid with yourself and expressed exactly what each piece means to *you.* You should be proud of yourself for doing the work many are unwilling to confront, and I hope that feels gratifying as well.

As a final, and optional, opportunity to really drive this chart home, feel free to write in your own words in the areas shared by two circles and not touching the third (the spaces where two of the three inner circles overlap, between the growth ingredients and growth itself). If you choose to get this granular, what you add can serve as a powerful reminder of what going all in looks like. For example, in the space where grace and gratitude intersect but grit is not included, you might write something like *"blissfully broken,"* meaning that, without grit, you're in a good headspace but not compelled to action and thus not operable in your purpose.

Doing this for all three partial intersections can be clarifying or confusing, so I'll leave it to you to decide. There may also be value in leaving these fields open for now and filling them in later as you find yourself partially engaged and arriving at the words that name what you're feeling in that state.

Cheers! May you grow through what you go through.

MY ENVIVO GROWTH CHART

My relentless *endeavor* is

I maintain *neutral thinking* by

My big three core *values* are

My vocational *interest* is

My *vision* for the future entails

I manage my relationship to *outcomes* by pursuing impact that looks like

---

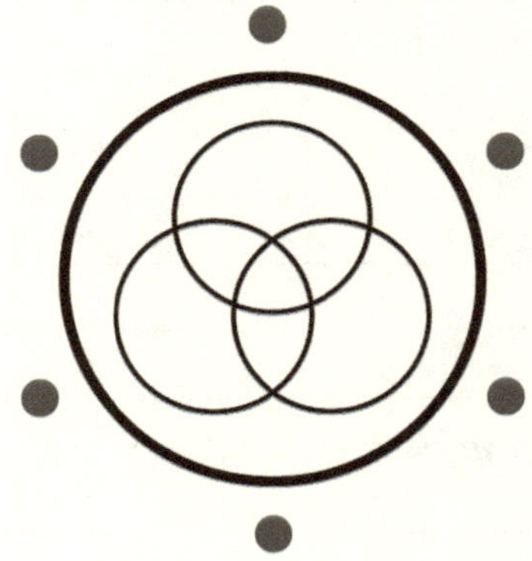

MY GROWTH INGREDIENTS:

I show *grace* to myself and others by

____

____

____

I employ *grit* by doing the work of

____

____

____

I express *gratitude* daily by

____

____

____

As these elements align in my life, I experience *growth*.

PART THREE
DWELLING IN CONFIDENT CADENCE

You've engaged in meaningful practices to excavate purpose and bravely choose growth. You should be proud of all the work you've done to this point!

Now we shift from all the doing to the *being*. Of course, a part of our being involves our doing, but there's a rich reality to explore in finding a respite from chronic doing.

A high achiever doesn't have to be an overachiever. A person rooted in purpose and empowered in growth knows when to clock out and turn in. The mature soul finds peace in a full night's rest without being haunted by the pressures of productivity. The wisest among us understand, in full clarity, that when we proactively recharge, we powerfully re-engage. Ironically and beautifully, we journey further faster when we make room for our rhythm to roll slower.

In the pages that follow, we'll find a cadence to carry confidently, a safe standard in our striving that primes us for longevity. We'll challenge the belief of the Type A person who lives a green-light lifestyle, and also the Type B person who prefers the red-light lifestyle. We'll lean into the truth of middle-ground moments, a yellow-light lifestyle. We'll ask and answer the question: what does it look like to not speed nor stall, but to patiently and practically honor the rhythm of the road?

Let's dive in! Enjoy the journey.

CHAPTER 11
A DELICATE DANCE

There is a rhythm between rigor and rest.

Hustle & Flow is arguably the greatest movie title of all time. While the quality of the plot is debatable and it didn't exactly ace its Rotten Tomatoes score, the *title* is supreme. I like the mantra-like movement of those words and what they can come to mean if we carry them as a banner while pursuing a life in rhythm. If you're all hustle, you'll eventually break down. If you're all flow, you'll never break through. To honor "Hustle & Flow" would mean, then, that we hold both pieces of the matrix in high regard and hone a skill for wielding them well in proper proportion.

Consider the artful ampersand. The iconic symbol doesn't stop at representing the word "and," complementing a written block of text gorgeously, as it does in this title. The ampersand also represents nuance, the joining of separate and independent parts to form one cohesive whole. We need more ampersands in our lives so we become more "yes and" and less "no but," and we can consider the new flow we'd find in a life lived beyond our self-imposed boundaries.

When being formed into your best self, you can't flip a light switch up and grind away at growth principles like there's an uncomplicated linear path to achievement. Likewise, you can't afford to flip a switch down, putting off purpose work for later, hoping you'll someday happen to feel like it.

The same can be said for establishing a viable pace for the life you're building, to which you'll apply these practices. Developing a dimmer-switch mentality is priceless, as it allows you to scan your environment and know intuitively when to smoothly shift higher into focused effort and when to dial down deeper into recovery. No obsession. No abandonment. Simple consistency. Ride the wave. Remember, both grace and grit are core elements in your approach to growth.

Don't be surprised when you feel yourself leaning to one end of the spectrum over the other. For some of us, there's a hardwired underlying inclination that pulls us in one direction. You may already have strong thoughts on this or easily identify with a Type A or Type B personality. This is normal and natural. For others, an effort is underway to achieve a more harmonious approach, but we discover the communication pool is contaminated. The middle ground is flooded. Rival social stances contaminate the messages around us. This can drive us into a divisive standoff, encouraging us to exclusively honor one side of the conversation and undervalue any thought to the contrary.

There's a culture war in digital discourse. One population of gurus on screens pushes a hardline hustle culture, insisting that we don't get what we want in life because we aren't willing to put in the sweat it takes to succeed. Ranging from sincere to brash, they've all got a certainty in their stance, a lavish lifestyle as proof of concept, and convincing statistics to back it further, coaxing you to follow their lead.

On the other end, we see a multitude advocating for rest as a form of resilience, a powerful means of taking a nonconformist angle against a capitalistic world. Again, what we see here are strong arguments, compelling statistical data suggesting that hustle culture is killing us sooner, and a very logically persuasive tug to follow their lead.

So, what's true in all of this? The inconvenient answer is that both sides have their hands in some tainted truth, making room for both credit and criticism. Both share one side of what's real, with neither properly validating the truth spoken on the side they haven't chosen. Humans need to strive, *and* humans need to sleep.

As we search for confirmation bias and create algorithmic echo chambers, we take in some toxic cheerleading, convincing us that we are right, that anyone who disagrees is an idiot, and that the world would be a better place if everyone aligned with our chosen perspective. What we root for, we begin to believe is true. This defies logic, as preference does not determine prevalence.

One great example of this fallacy playing out can be found in our track record of electing U.S. presidents. In every electoral cycle, millions of people head to the polls, with many voting left and many voting right. Major media outlets, claiming neutrality, take part by firing up one base or the other, furthering the tribalistic rift in groupthink. Two predominant camps rally: red versus blue. Each side is believed to be far superior to the other by large and similar percentages of the population.

Despite all this effort and passion, at the time of this writing, it has been thirty-two years since we've had two presidents in a row from the same party. That's over three decades of seeing a consistent pattern of power shifting back and forth across the aisle. Billions of dollars are raised, support groups are organized, feral emotions are expressed, wounding words and misinformation are widespread, families are even torn apart on holidays over this stuff… And yet, as a collective, we continue riding the same rhythmic wave.

Tribalism doesn't change the truth. There is a pendulum swinging right to left, left to right, with no regard for your opinion or mine. This is not to say that we shouldn't practice our civic duty to vote, but rather that we should perhaps revisit the earlier chapter regarding the importance of releasing our attachment to outcomes. Furthermore, we have to accept the fact that whatever side we wish wasn't in the equation does, in fact, make up half the equation.

Embracing the ampersand means we ditch the black-and-white thinking and allow our world to be colored by nuance. We cannot sustain a stop-and-go life as if there are no yellow lights. Going all or nothing means we don't get to accomplish *something*. The key to success is knowing which end of the spectrum you naturally fall on and being willing to cross the aisle to make peace with the whole of your existence.

Rhythm looks like a life that honors your Type A penchant for the grind and also makes space to unwind. Rhythm is a Type B lifestyle that honors a cadence of rest and also rises to the test. For both sides, a life in rhythm is the great unifier of human vitality, granting us all the power and permission to *work from a position of rest.*

Yes, you read that right. We ought to work from a position of rest.

Consider the case studies we've examined and notice the trend. The quarterback in the clutch needs a mind at rest while his body is in motion. The bison fights the storm to find rest in the sunshine. The loblolly seed lies passively, disregarded and buried in the mud, before it towers into the sky.

Even the way we, as humans, interact with our environment echoes this truth. Trees emit oxygen in what biologically resembles an exhale. Humans inhale this and then exhale carbon dioxide. Trees inhale the carbon dioxide, begetting the birth of more oxygen, and on and on the cycle goes. Imagine that… two different life forms, each generously and involuntarily empowering the other to long-term sustainability.

Abundance flows in the give-and-take of ordinary rhythms. If we are to honor the ENVIVO Method to decipher purpose and then lean into grace, grit, and gratitude to step into growth, we must submit to the natural, sacred tempo our lives were designed to honor.

We'll close by taking a look at the concept of eustress. Across decades of studies, the research is conclusive and clear. Exhaustive trials have shown that eustress, defined as moderately intense physical and psychological stress, is fundamentally good for human flourishing.

I love the word "moderately." It has some "ampersand" to it: challenge yourself, *and* don't burn yourself out. There's something in that for both the Type A person who is burning the candle at both ends and the Type B person who sits long in contemplation, considering whether it is yet time to buy the matches. The truth lives in the messy middle.

It's time to rewrite your rhythm. Notice that you never have to ask if music is out of rhythm. You hear it sharply. Dissonance, or a lack of harmony, is an unpleasant attack on your ears. You immediately wish to change the tune. In the same way, you don't have to ask if your life is out of rhythm. You feel it sharply. It's unpleasant. This is an open invitation to change the tune.

Welcome, eustress. Work the dimmer switch. Honor the ampersand. Dwelling in confident cadence looks like finding your sweet spot between the parts of truth you're innately drawn to and the parts that draw the best out of you. Here's one way to frame it: What mildly stresses you wildly stretches you. Set a goal just outside your comfort zone, and watch your capacity grow to meet it.

As a final journaling practice, take space outside of this book in a separate journal or notepad to reflect and write. Your journal entry may be long and descriptive or short and succinct. Follow your natural inclination to draw it forward clearly. Prompts are provided here, the answers to which will lead you toward writing the exact guiding words *you* need, something I cannot give you, nor can any coach or book.

Using any wisdom gained here, apply your answers in a deeply personal way. Within your writing, nine of your sentences will begin with softly scripted language, guided by the prompts provided. Write out these prompts and then finish the sentence with your goal-aligned answers. After completing this closing exercise, notice the confidence you feel, knowing that you've brought things into full form with some independence instead of being told what to do.

It's time to lean into intuition, take ownership, and then build a structure that carries you toward a wonderful life of fulfillment. As the ancient Roman emperor and Stoic philosopher Marcus Aurelius put it, "Love the discipline you know and let it support you." Do not fill in the blanks here. Your brain records the information better when your hand physically writes these sentences out completely. This can be several pages long, crafted as a letter to yourself, with the prompt responses sprinkled throughout, along with other thoughts that solidify your game plan. It can also be short, with you simply writing out the prompts yourself and then completing each thought as you also write out the answers to them.

Find a quiet moment and an uncluttered space; turn on your low-stimulation, lyric-free music, or simply enjoy silence. No rushing allowed; take time to settle into this one. What comes forward in your writing here will become the cadence to which you live out your walk in purpose and growth.

Remember, it's not sluggish, nor is it savage. It's *sustainable.* This is a life in rhythm.

I will incorporate the ENVIVO Method and get clear on my life purpose by ____

____

The hardest principle in the ENVIVO method for me is ____________________, and I will intentionally challenge myself to honor and embrace it by ______________________________

____

I will practice grace for myself and others by __________________

____

I will lean into grit, when I don't feel like it, by _______________

____

I will prioritize gratitude by __________________________

____

I will cultivate self-awareness of my rhythm of rigor and rest by

____

____

I will use this awareness to change my tempo by (list practical practices you will add or remove) __________________________

____

I will begin this new life rhythm by (date) __________________

____

I will be held accountable by (name a person or community)

____

____

CONCLUSION

Purpose looks like knowing who you're here to be and deducing from that what you're here to do. Growth looks like leaning into the hard thing to unlock the good thing. Rhythm looks like finding the right cadence from which to practice your purpose and pursue your growth, making space for the rigor *and* the rest.

All of these elements look good on you. When these three guiding virtues align and you carry them confidently, you shine at your best and brightest. You embody the hustle *and* honor the flow. Unhurried and unanxious, you cultivate your calling.

Beyond the book, there's the becoming. Pause and mindfully ask yourself: *What will become possible for me as I hold these principles and apply them? What hindrances will now fall away? What new superpowers will now be added to me? How will I be transformed by the renewing of my mind?*

This is only the first leg on a brilliant new lifelong journey. I've begun a conversation with you that never has to end. May you continue to ask big questions, delight in the answers that surface, and forever continue learning, feeling, reframing, and growing. Every word written here is merely a preface. Now it's time for you to write the remainder of your story.

Enjoy the journey.

THANK YOU FOR READING LIFE IN RHYTHM!

Just to say thanks for buying and reading my book, I would like to give you a free bonus gift, no strings attached!
Scan the QR Code for a free video masterclass:

I appreciate your interest in Life in Rhythm and value your feedback, as it helps me improve future versions.
Please leave your invaluable review on Amazon.com with your thoughts.
Thank you!

www.ingramcontent.com/pod-product-compliance
Lightning Source LLC
LaVergne TN
LVHW090525110826
845146LV00003B/979